THE

Theory and Practice of Human Magnetism.

Translated from the French of

H. DURVILLE

(JOURNAL DU MAGNETISME)

Reprint 2016 facsimile
ISBN-13: 978-1537524436
ISBN-10: 1537524437

PUBLISHED BY
THE PSYCHIC RESEARCH COMPANY,
TIMES-HERALD BUILDING,
CHICAGO.

Reprint 2016 facsimile
ISBN-13: 978-1537524436
ISBN-10: 1537524437

PREFACE

BY THE

Publishers of the American Edition.

IN these days when Magnetic Healers of positive and negative ability are inflicting their courses of instruction upon the public at prices ranging from $5.00 to $100.00, courses of instruction which are neither more nor less than "rot" from cover to cover, there is a real need for a popular work bearing upon the subject of Magnetic Healing in all its branches from the hand of one who is at least a scholar and a master of his profession. Thank God, here's the book! Price $1.00.

INTRODUCTION

By the Author.

A good practitioner ought to have not only a theory enabling him to explain as nearly as possible the effects which he observes, but he should also know the theories of the Masters who have gone before. In order that future practitioners may select a theory already laid down, or what is preferable, that they may, after research, experiments, and comparisons, form a personal one of their own, it is indispensable for me to develop my theory. That is what I will do in a very few words.

PART I.

THE THEORY OF MAGNETISM.

I. *General Physics.* Theory of emission, dynamic theory. Movement, ether and natural forces; transformation of forces. II. *Magnetism.* Magnetic force, its action, its transmission from one person to another, the action of movement. III. *The art of magnetising.* Divers considerations. How to become a magnetiser. IV. *Physical laws of human magnetism.* Popularity. Remarks.

The Theory and Practice

OF

HUMAN MAGNETISM

———

CONTENTS.

PART I.

CHAPTER I.

My theory of magnetism reposes exclusively on the data of general physics. It is based on the effects produced by the magnetic force, a force, the existence of which, under divers names, was known in the remotest antiquity to a numerous category of learned observers; notwithstanding which fact, it has never been formally accepted by official science.

All the writers on the natural sciences considered magnetism as a special force of the human body; and comparing this force with the forces or agents observable in nature, they explained its action by the theories of physics which were in vogue in their day.

During the last century and even up to the middle of the present, the action of the natural forces was explained by the emission of special fluids called imponderable fluids, which escaped from the body and radiated at a distance. That was the *theory of emission*. Then they had a caloric fluid to explain the action of heat, a luminous fluid to explain the action of light, two

7

fluids, a southern and a northern, were separated from each other in the magnet; and the same was the case with electricity, which had its positive and negative fluid.

Following this theory, the magnetisers all adopted the existence of a particular fluid special to the human body, namely, a *magnetic fluid,* which, radiating around us, passed from one individual to another, as heat, light, electricity and magnetism (special to the loadstone) pass from one body to the other in certain of their manifestations. This principle served as a basis for all the theories of magnetism set forth, from Paracelsus down to Du Potet and Lafontaine; and we readily conceived that it could not be otherwise.

The science of the present day no longer explains the action of natural forces by the emission of fluids, however imponderable one might imagine them, because these fluids do not and cannot exist, since heat, light, electricity and magnetism (of the loadstone) are only special forms, transformations of movement, that is, manifestations of energy. The unity of nature's forces is demonstrated most indisputably, and the mechanism of their transformations is explained by means of a new theory; the *dynamic* or *wave theory.*

In determined conditions, the presence of one

of the natural forces, heat, light, electricity, magnetism (special to the loadstone) produces one or even several others; in other words, they generate each other, and each one of them can change itself into all the others. A few examples will suffice to bring to the memory these transformations, which we constantly observe, but to which we scarcely pay any attention.

If a rod of iron be placed in an ardent furnace, it is soon seen that the *heat* is communicated from one to the other. The rod is heated more and more, and soon its heat from being dark becomes luminous; it first gets *red,* then *white,* and produces *light.* In the locomotive and various machines heat is transformed into *mechanical movement.* In a circuit suitably arranged heat produces the electric current which, in its turn gives us *magnetization, light, mechanical movement* and *chemical analysis.*

An analysis of light will produce *colors,* and in these we observe *chemical action,* and *caloric action;* moreover, *heat* is inseparable from light in conditions where, in nature, light impresses our retina. You can always have proof of this by using a differential thermometer, or, better still, with a Melloni pile, in the circuit of which *electric currents* are produced.

Electricity circulating in a conductor determines *heat.* If the current is intense, or if any resistance whatever should interpose in the conductor, that is, a body offering difficulty in being traversed by the current, the point of this resistance heated beyond measure, becomes luminous; the heat which had been obscure, becomes visible in the form of *light*. That is the principle of electric lighting. The electric current also produces motive force, i. e., *mechanical movement* and likewise *chemical analysis*. If we place a bar of iron or steel across an electric current, this bar becomes magnetised and produces the phenomena of *magnetism* which are described in physics. This is the principle on which reposes the construction of the electro-magnets which are used, among other purposes, in our electric bells.

Magnetism (proper to the loadstone) placed near a circuit under certain conditions of displacement, develops *electric currents*. It is upon this principle that the construction of the dynamos which give us *light* and motive power reposes, that is, *mechanical movement*. On the other hand, *mechanical movement* and *chemical analysis* produce *heat* and *electricity* with which again, we obtain *light, magnetism*, etc., etc.

At first sight it would seem as if these different agents transform themselves into each other, but more careful attention enables us to observe that there is only one transformation of movement. Thus, the electric current, for example, is a movement caused and maintained by a force of some kind. If there is production of heat by the electric current, it is that, by the action of electricity, the atoms of the bodies in which this electricity circulates are put in motion, and this molecular motion constitutes *heat*. From this it will readily be understood that it is not electricity itself, but only the movement of electricity which is transformed into heat. In the same way when an electric current is formed under the action of heat, it is not the formation of electricity which takes place, but only the starting in action of the electricity contained in the conductors ; heat is changed into electrical motion.

Now, what is *movement?*

Everything which moves, oscillates, vibrates, balances, stirs, changes position, goes or transports itself from one point to another is in movement. Movement is everywhere, it is one of the essential elements of the life of the universe. The stars which are eternally gravitating are in motion. All the animals on the surface of the earth, from the microbe and the infusory, to the thinking being arrived at the highest degree of perfection which we can conceive, are in movement. The constituent elements of the atmosphere in which hurricanes rage are always in motion and disturb everything that exists on the face of the earth. Our imperfect senses can always directly perceive conspicuous, plain movement, the movement or motion of bodies themselves. But bodies are composed of molecules, and molecules themselves are formed of agglomerated atoms, separated from each other by relatively enormous spaces in which they move. This movement of the atoms of bodies changes continually because it receives and transmits the impulsion which it receives from without by the intermediary of ether.

What is *ether?*

Ether is a hypothetical fluid and the only one which contemporary physics has retained. It is the "soul of the world" of the Peripatetics, the "universal fluid" of the magnetisers of the 17th and 18th centuries. It is the representation of matter in the most subtle state it is possible to imagine. Extremely elastic, and having no other property of its own than that of transmitting the changes of movement, it fills the entire universe, in placing the stars in communication with each other by the light which they send one another reciprocally, by attraction, gravitation and probably by certain other forces of which we have no knowledge as yet. It fills the interatomic spaces of bodies, and enables atoms to impart their own special movement, or to transmit that which they receive from without, from one place to another within a certain radius.

Returning after this digression to movement, we find that the movement of atoms is a vibratory one, and so extremely rapid that, in a given time, it is capable of attaining a number of vibrations which appalls the imagination. As an example, I extract from an address by William Crookes to the Society for Psychical Research of London, in 1897, the following data laid down by that illustrious physicist, who took for his starting point the pendulum beating seconds in air, and kept on doubling these oscillations.

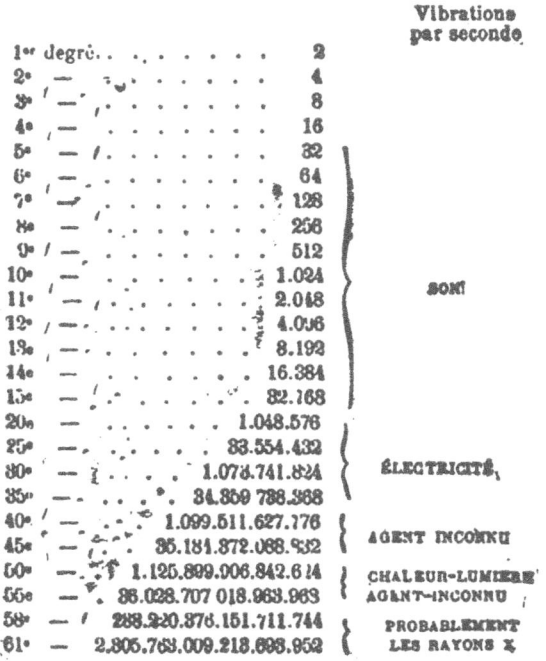

	Vibrations per seconde
1er degré	2
2° —	4
3° —	8
4° —	16
5° —	32
6° —	64
7° —	128
8° —	256
9° —	512
10° —	1.024
11° —	2.048
12° —	4.096
13° —	8.192
14° —	16.384
15° —	32.168
20° —	1.048.576
25° —	33.554.432
30° —	1.073.741.824
35° —	34.859.788.368
40° —	1.099.511.627.776
45° —	35.184.372.088.932
50° —	1.125.899.906.842.614
55° —	36.028.707.018.963.963
58° —	288.230.376.151.711.744
61° —	2.305.763.009.213.693.952

Right-hand brackets labels: SON ; ÉLECTRICITÉ ; AGENT INCONNU ; CHALEUR-LUMIÈRE AGENT-INCONNU ; PROBABLEMENT LES RAYONS X

At the fifth step from unity, continues Crookes, at 32 vibrations per second, we reach the region where the atmospheric vibration reveals itself to us in the form of sound. Here we have the lowest musical note. In the next ten steps the vibrations per second rise from 32 to 32,768, and here, to the average human ear, the region of sound ends. But certain more highly endowed animals probably hear sounds too acute for our organs, that is, sounds which vibrate at a higher rate.

We next enter a region in which the vibrations rise rapidly, and the vibrating medium is no longer the gross atmosphere, but a highly attenuated medium, "a diviner air" called the ether. From the 16th to the 36th step, the vibrations rise from 32,768 to 34,359,738,368 per second, such vibrations appearing to our means of observation as electrical rays. We next reach a region extending from the 35th to the 45th step, including from 34,359,738,368 to 35,184,372,-088,832 vibrations per second. This region may be considered as unknown, because we are as yet ignorant what are the functions of vibrations of the rates just mentioned. But that they have some function it is fair to suppose. Now we approach the region of light, the steps extending from the 45th to between the 50th and 51st and the vibrations extending from 35,184,372,088,832 per second (heat rays) to 1,875,000,000,000,000 per second, the highest recorded rays of the spectrum. The actual sensation of light, and therefore, the vibrations which transmit visible signs, being comprised between the narrow limits of about 450,000,000,000,000 (red light) and 750,000,000,000,000 (violet light) less than one step.

Leaving the region of visible light, we arrive at what is, for our existing senses and our means of research, another unknown region, the functions of which we are beginning to suspect. It is not unlikely that the X rays of Professor Roentgen will be found to lie between the 58th and 61st steps having vibrations extending from 288,220,376,151,711,744 to 2,305,763,009,213,-693,952 per second or even higher.

In this series it will be seen there are two great gaps, or unknown regions concerning which we must own our entire ignorance as to the part they play in the economy of creation. Further, whether any vibrations exist having a greater number per second than those classes mentioned, we do not presume to decide."

These vibrations are transmitted to the ether by waves in a manner not unlike the motion we see on the surface of calm water into which a stone is thrown. But the motions are not identical, because not only do they vary in speed, but also in form and amplitude, and their waves are longer. As we have just seen in the table established by the learned Englishman, it is these vibrations which produce the natural forces. Thus, certain vibrations of a specific nature produce *heat*, others more rapid produce *light*, others varying in speed form and amplitude produce *electricity*, *magnetism* (proper to the loadstone) and the *magnetism* which is the subject of this work.

CHAPTER II.

MAGNETIC FORCE:—ITS ACTION:—TRANSMISSION OF FROM ONE TO ANOTHER—THE ACTION OF MOVEMENT.

Notwithstanding the aridity of the subject, which belongs to the highest problems of general physics, I think I have set before the reader enough fundamental ideas to enable him to understand the mechanism of the wave theory which serves at the present time to explain the action of nature's forces, and more particularly those of heat, light, electricity and magnetism (of the loadstone). Now let us see how this theory is going to help us to explain the effects of the force which I have called physiological magnetism, for the reason that it acts on the organism without influencing the magnetic needle.

To begin with, physiological magnetism, like all the forces which are usually called *nature's agents*, is a form of movement, a manifestation of energy: and this special force observed in the human body and whose action ancient magnetisers explained by the communication of an imponderable fluid, which they called *magnetic fluid*, is (as already claimed by Puységur and Deleuze) only *the action, or virtue, or elasticity of the movement* proper to all the functions of our organism.   This action, virtue or elasticity of movement without doubt consists of certain vibrations of the atoms forming the human body, vibrations, the nature, form, speed and mode of communication of which are entirely unknown to us.   It is this movement, transmitted in waves through the ether, from one individual to another, which constitutes what I call the *magnetic agent*.   It is therefore a purely physical agent, a legitimate brother of heat, light, electricity and all of nature's forces.

That which gives me the most absolute certainty that this agent is really a physical agent is that we everywhere observe, not only in the human body, but also in the animal and vegetable kingdoms, in inanimate bodies, in heat, in light, in static and dynamic forms of electricity, in the magnet, in terrestrial magnetism, in magnetism proper to the loadstone, in mechanical movement, in sound, in chemical analysis, even in odors, that it is everywhere subject to the same laws.

The form of the movement which produces physiological magnetism is therefore in everything and everywhere. It is undoubtedly the most universal force of nature that we can conceive and direct, as well at the bottom of the sea, the center of the earth or the highest strata of the atmosphere. Although official science has never acknowledged this scientific truth, it is notwithstanding the most apparent manifestation of atomic life, and although we possess no sense to perceive it directly, nothing is easier for whoever would, to account for its presence by the effects it determines on the organism.

What is the quickness of the vibrations which produce physiological magnetism? What is the length of the waves? Nobody knows, because the attention of the learned has not yet been directed to the subject. The task, although difficult, is not impossible of accomplishment, and certainly physicists of the future will be enabled to add to classical physics a complete chapter in which physiological magnetism will be demonstrated in the most rigorously scientific manner. Meanwhile everything tends to make me accept the theory that the movement which produces this force is found in Crookes table, in one of the two gaps, the functions of whose vibrations are not yet known, and more especially in the last, that is, in the region extending from the 50th to 55th steps, there where the frequency of the vibrations attains 36,028,707,018,963,968 per second.

I will not pursue further the comparisons to be established between physiological magnetism and the other natural forces, thinking it sufficient to have demonstrated the analogy which exists between them, showing their relationship and connection; and of my readers for whom these considerations may be too advanced, I subjoin the following account of human magnetism which Mesmer and his followers called *Animal Magnetism*.

The atoms constituting the various parts of the human body are continually executing vibratory movements, the nature of which is not known to us, in other words and to use an expression easy of comprehension, the human body vibrates in a certain manner, and this vibratory motion constitutes *human magnetism*.

This essentially physical movement is conveyed from one person to another, the same as the movement of terrestrial magnetism is conveyed to the magnetic needle, or from one magnet to another magnet, or better still, like the movement of a warm body to a body or to a medium less warm. An example will make this clear. A warm body, let us say a lighted stove, is placed in a cold room. The atoms from the stove vibrate in a certain manner, and this vibratory movement produces heat. This heat, which is one of the forms of movement, is then conveyed by waves from point to point in the aerial medium, in a space of time as short as the energy constituting the source of heat is proportionately great. Then the room gets warm, and all bodies or persons in it participate in this warmth, which becomes general, all the sooner because they are good conductors of heat. An equilibrium of temperature sets in, and exists to a considerable extent between the warm body, that is, the lighted stove which produces this heat, and the ethereal medium, that is, the room and the bodies or individuals in it, and the movement constituting the heat becomes general by spreading everywhere.

Human magnetism is conveyed in a similar manner, with this difference only, that, in a great many cases, as in the effects of transmission of thought, sympathy or antipathy which we feel toward a person whom we approach for the first time, the transmission is much more rapid. In any case, whatever the rapidity with which this transmission is produced we may frequently notice it in the ordinary conditions of everyday life. Here are a few examples:

Certain needs which we satisfy excite among
those around us similar needs. You no sooner
laugh or yawn than several others feel the need
of laughing or yawning. If you are gloomy and
depressed, and you go among people who all are
happy and contented, you soon become cheerful.
And likewise, the reverse takes place under opposite conditions. A man having a profound con-
viction (whether justified by reason, or based on
an illusion of his mind, makes no difference provided it be genuine) acts upon those around him,
and makes fanatics of them like himself. Almost
all zealous adherents of political and religious
sects have no other means of subjecting men, per-
verting their intelligence and submitting them to
their despotism. In the theater, an actor thoroughly imbued with his part, imagining himself
to be the real hero he is representing, wakes fear,
terror or admiration in the spectators, who become impressed, laugh or cry as the case may be,
although they are well aware the scene before
them is only a creation of the intelligence. We
all know that example is contagious; joy and sorrow, virtue and vice, health and sickness are all
transmitted. Popular belief justifies this truth in
the proverb, "Tell me the company you keep, and
I will tell you who you are." This communication of movement, this transmission which operates like the heat of the lighted stove does in the

aerial medium, is certainly the cause of disturbances by mobs, uprisings of the populace, and many other acts which we may notice in a concourse or assembly of people. Proof of this communication may be seen in the propagation of certain contagious diseases and affections, and in those where the nervous system, as in hysteria for example, is more particularly affected. The physiologist, not usually understanding the mechanism of this communication, attributes it to *imitation,* not realizing that here imitation is but the effect of a cause which he overlooks.

Here are a few more examples not less conclusive. Thought, which is elaborated in the depths of the cerebral mass, can be transmitted from one person to another, and is a form of *mental suggestion.* I have more than once sat opposite a person I know, and an idea occurring to me has been reflected in that person, and if I have told him the subject of my thought I have often obtained an answer like this: "I was thinking of what you tell me, and was just going to speak to you about it." The explanation of this phenomenon is very simple:

When the soul thinks, is pleased or suffers, a vibratory movement of the brain is produced, which is identical in all brains for the same thought, the same desire, the same requirement; in fine, for the same manner of being of the individuals. This movement, which is conveyed to the nervous system, is not extinguished at the ends of the nerves, but is transmitted by waves to the aerial medium. These waves strike the nervous system of persons placed in the sphere of their action, and traveling along the length of the nerves without change, the vibratory movement reaches the brain, where the same thought, the same desire, the same want, or the same manner of being, is reproduced automatically. This transmission is all the easier and more complete when the receiving subject is more impressionable, more *sensitive*. A feeble, sickly person borrows energy from the strong and robust persons around him. It is for this reason that the child is so happy in its mother's arms, and that the sick and convalescent, exhausted by long spells of suffering, experience feelings of alleviation, relief and comfort when in the presence of a sympathetic friend. The results caused by transmission of this nature are innumerable. It is sufficient to watch ourselves and others, to study the nature of the sensations which we feel in the various circumstances of everyday life to be soon convinced that the greatest number of phenomena which we improperly attribute to hazard are due to one cause, namely, *the converse influence which individuals involuntarily exercise upon each other.* This influence is felt in pursuance of the communication of the action of the movement of the different persons, which action of movement, variable at first, tends to become unified and similar in all the persons of a group or assembly.

This is a form of *human magnetism* which may be termed *involuntary magnetism*. If we observe what takes place among animals we see results similar to those produced among human beings. Naturalists tell us that certain animals feel the approach of their enemies from considerable distances; that the wolf exerts a certain power upon the dog at a distance of many miles and causes him to howl, and we all know that the serpent from the foot of a tree fascinates the bird reposing on its top and attracts it to him and devours it, and that the hawk from a great height often deprives the timid lark of all power of motion. And all these actions have no other cause than that which permits men, consciously or unconsciously, to act upon each other. It is a communication of movement imposed by the strong upon the weak; and the weaker intimidated, fascinated and mastered by the successive waves of the force which takes hold of him, engrosses, clasps him and places his life in danger, finally feels all the horror of his situation. This is a form of *magnetism of animals*.

If we direct our attention to the vegetable

kingdom we notice the same resemblance. The attraction which members of the male sex exercise upon those of the female sex is very great both in the vegetable and animal kingdoms, and this attraction is particularly noticeable in plants at the time they are adorned with all the attributes of beauty, youth and strength, when they array themselves to accomplish the act of generation indispensable to the perpetuation of the species. In unisexual flowers, that is; in those where the pistil and the stamens are on different flowers, such as the willow, corn, melon, and all the cucurbitaceæ, you can almost always see the stamen flowers incline toward the pistils in order to deposit there the fecundating pollen, and the pistils, not less amiable and complaisant, likewise bend down to the former so as to receive the vital principle offered them. This attraction is still more remarkable in certain species where the stamen flowers (males) and the pistil flowers (females) are on different stalks, such as hemp, etc. This reciprocity of action is constituted by a communication of movement established from a flower or stalk of one sex to a flower or stalk of another sex; and this communication is a form of *vegetable magnetism.*

Striking analogous cases are also observed in the mineral kingdom. All metals are susceptible of acting upon us, and, in some manner, of

modifying our conduct and mode of existence, that is, by increasing or diminishing our
organic activity. This action is determined by a
particular vibratory movement of the atoms of
each metal, a motion which by means of successive waves is communicated to our movement and
eventually modifies it. This action of metals
which has been successfully employed under the
name of metallotherapy by Drs. Burg and Moni-
court, in the treatment of certain nervous affections, constitutes in the plainest and most indisputable manner, *mineral magnetism.*

On the other hand, chemists are aware that
atoms of metals are attracted, united and agglomerated in the middle of the earth in order
to form molecules, which in their turn form ores,
nuggets, gold dust, etc.

Two musical strings placed near each other in
tension, will vibrate in unison when only one is
put in movement. Two pendulums of equal
length suspended near each other on the same
plane of oscillation and started in motion together, continue to oscillate, when the oscillating
movement is only kept up in one of them. This
phenomenon occurs even where the two pendulums are separated by a wall. In the most com-
prehensive, apparent, visible fashion, this phenomenon is nothing but a communication, a transmission of the movement of one pendulum to

the other. This is the *magnetism of mechanical movement,* which can even be transmitted through a medium which is solid, but which is impenetrable by light and electricity and only slightly penetrable by heat.

Like electric currents, electrified bodies are attracted or repulsed at a distance, and the action of electricity employed in therapeutics in a certain way constitutes the *magnetism of electricity.*

At first it would appear as if the magnet offered phenomena analogous to those of electricity. At a distance, two magnets oppose each other when they are brought together by their same poles, they are attracted to each other when they are brought together by their opposite poles. At a distance the properties of the magnet are communicated to certain metals, such as iron and steel, nickel, cobalt, chrome, and these are transformed into veritable magnets. A magnet having an elongated form like the needle of a compass, and suspended or poised on a pivot, points in the direction of the meridian, obeying that form of movement which I have designated by the name of *terrestrial magnetism.* These combined properties of magnets, the philosophers designated by the general name of magnetism, but I am obliged to call it *magnetism peculiar to the magnet* in order to distinguish it from the magnetism which we see everywhere in nature and which is the subject of these comparisons. Permit me to say, that in the magnet we observe two forces, two different agents which we can dissociate from each other and study separately, namely, *physical force*, known to the philosophers, and *physiological* force, which was entirely unknown to them. The latter is similar and almost identical with the magnetic force we observe in the human body, in animals, in plants, and in all bodies or natural forces; it is subject to the same physical laws. It is this force, this agent, and the various forms of its movement, which constitute what we call today the *magnetic force*.

Briefly, we see that everything obeys a mysterious force the nature of which is unknown to us, and to which we might give the name of *universal movement*. The heavenly bodies which gravitate in space are attracted toward each other in direct ratio of their magnitude, and in inverse ratio of the square of their distance. The influence of the sun and the moon is felt in the movement of the sea, and produces the flux and reflux of the tide. This influence is equally felt on the health of mankind, on the growth of plants and on everything that lives on the surface of the earth. The odors of plants may cause us joy, sorrow, sickness or even death. Finally, we see that everything in nature is linked together by laws which subordinate causes to effects, and that everything proves that there exists between the various bodies or agents of nature, a continuous exchange of *movement,* or, if you prefer it, I will say of atoms, effluvia or "fluids" which renders the one tributary to the other. General movement, which we may here style *universal magnetism,* modified by the movement special to each body or natural force constitutes a particular magnetism, just as the movement of the human body which is the subject of our present inquiry constitutes, human or physiological magnetism, in abbreviation—Magnetism.

CHAPTER III.

THE ART OF MAGNETIZING—DIVERS CONDITIONS— HOW TO BECOME A MAGNETIZER.

The principal basis of the physical theory of *human magnetism* being established, we will now say a few words concerning a higher and more transcendental magnetism, viz., *psychic magnetism,* which certainly holds, as well as the first, a place of considerable importance. Admitting within us the presence of a psychic element, let us say, the soul, we are bound to admit that this element exercises an external action from soul to soul, and probably from a soul to a strange body. The soul must vibrate, and its movement of vibration which is very rapid must (like the vibrations of bodies composed of matter which is apparent to our senses) be communicated by waves in the ethereal medium, in the ether, or in a still more subtle fluid. Notwithstanding the analogies which we seem to foresee, we can only hazard hypotheses, because absolutely nothing is known about the laws which regulate the action of psychical magnetism. But it is clear that certain individuals do exercise a power at a distance, and that thought, desire and will power appear to be the principal motors of this action. Possibly waves of a particular nature originating in the psychic body are impelled with velocity in a given direction far beyond the limits which the waves proceeding from the action of our physical movement could attain.

Some practitioners, in the front ranks of whom I place the healing mediums, often obtain excellent results without observing any of the rules of physiological magnetism. They limit themselves to meditation, to proceeding along the lines of thought, prayer, calling to their assistance strange beings—spirits—who, they say, furnish them with the "fluids" which they need. I am perfectly convinced that healers of this kind are highly gifted magnetizers "having a good deal of fluid" as they used to say 50 years ago, and while retaining their belief which is perhaps of use to them, in putting themselves into a state of excitation, that is, to determine in them the movement special to their action, they would obtain far more considerable results if, in applying their principles they were to observe the physical laws which I have set forth. But I will not stop at these considerations which cannot convince the healers, because they remain and will doubtless remain a long time yet in their blind faith and unlimited confidence in the complaisance of the "good spirits" which often haunt their imagination.

While recognizing a *psychic mesmerism* which no one can deny, there yet remains the purely physical theory of *physiological magnetism* which explains to us in a clear manner the action of matter upon matter, and that of the human body upon another individual. A few physical and physiological considerations are still necessary. Atoms, or to speak in terms clear to everybody, the various parts of the human organism vibrating continually—the form of this movement which constitutes the magnetic force, is continually escaping from us, and in successive waves, is communicated to the ethereal medium, to ether, and from there to the individuals placed in its sphere of action. But it is good to bear in mind that the action most individuals exercise upon each other is not very intense. We do meet occasionally individuals of powerful athletic build whose waves are so strong that, in spite of themselves, they impress all those around them, but cases of this kind are exceptional. Properly speaking, magnetic force exists in all persons without exception, but beside the athletes of magnetism, there are the feeble, languishing or sickly, whose waves can scarcely be transmitted, and they need a tone of movement from external sources; they are, on account of their nature, almost incapable of communicating their own movement. Strong persons are rich in movement and *they can give*, whereas feeble individuals being poor in movement, in their own interest ought only *to receive* it. In addition to those who are strong and exercise a beneficial effect around them, there exist some strong persons who exert an injurious influence. I will only cite one example. An individual having the appearance of excellent physical and moral health marries. At the end of about 18 months or 2 years his partner falls sick, weakens and dies of an affection insufficiently characterized. The widower, not liking solitude, remarries, and at the end of a similar period of time he is again a widower, and will continue to be as often as he remarries. The individual unconsciously author of these cases of homicide is gifted with a pernicious action of movement which doubtless would exert upon himself a fatal effect if he did not exert it outside himself on innocent victims. Such cases are unusual, but a sufficient number are met with, as everybody is aware of their existence.

This transmission from the strong to the weak, from the man endowed with an energetic action of movement to the man deficient in it, is produced so simply and naturally that in most instances we hardly perceive its accomplishment but by the effects it determines in us, and for that it is necessary for us to think of the successive changes which our manner of living is subject to. Unknown to us, the movement which constitutes our magnetic personality is transmitted from one to another and tends to become equalized in the ethereal medium, like the level of a liquid in communicating vases. This manner of being, this movement which is communicated from one to another, is certainly magnetism, but an unconscious, involuntary magnetism which is considerably less powerful than artificial magnetism. There exists, therefore, a magnetic art which, with Lafontaine, we may call the *art of magnetizing*. In the exercise of this art, the adroitness of the operator is acquired after long practice and the study of scientific knowledge, but I will not speak of that here, remaining content with presenting a few observations not sufficiently emphasized already.

I think we understand that the intensity of the magnetic force must depend upon the number of vibrations that the atoms (constituent parts of the organism) execute in a second, that is, upon their precipitate or regular movement. And as a matter of fact there are times when we feel faint-hearted, dejected, without energy; then we do not vibrate *enough* to magnetize beneficially. On the other hand when we are renovated and overexcited, we *vibrate energetically* and we are conscious of this increase of activity by a well-defined internal agitation; then we can obtain in certain cases, much more important results than we can in a relatively calm state. Therefore, in order to increase his usual strength and to be in a condition to act perceptibly better than in the ordinary circumstances of life, the magnetiser ought to place himself in a special moral and physical disposition, a disposition similar to that he desires to obtain in his patient. He must especially place himself in a state of *activity, to give,* while his patient remains in a state of *passivity, to receive.*

How can he throw himself into that state? It is very simple to do, but somewhat difficult to explain. First of all, place yourself en rapport morally with your patient. This rapport is obtained by a fairly complex inward power by a sort of sympathy and compassion you have for your patient, by the intention and desire you have to heal, or at least relieve him. Then you concentrate his attention in a sort of isolation or meditation, as if to gather all his strength and power of action. If the patient needs excitation, as in the case of paralysis, or where there is only general debility, loss or diminution of muscular or vital energy, you throw yourself into a state of excitation or exaggeration of movement. You then feel yourself strong in order to increase in your patient the energy of his movement, and to raise it to the degree of elasticity it should have normally. If, on the other hand, the patient is laboring under great excitement, if he suffers violent pains, or from fever, the usual symptom of acute affections, his vibratory movement is too great, and you must reduce it, that is, calm it so as to get it back to its normal action; for this, you work yourself into a condition of repose, so as to transmit it to your patient.

Magnetic force of itself does not possess any therapeutic principle; its action on the human body is only that of an equilibriant. The healer must never try to do anything else than to equilibrate the patient's movement to his own. For this purpose, he must be able, at will, to increase or diminish the activity of his own movement, and give it the proper tone. The highly gifted operator easily gets accustomed, even at the start of his practice, to promptly bring himself of his own volition, into those special vibratory conditions which he wants to communicate. It will readily be seen that if will power serves any use in magnetizing, it does not, as was generally believed in former times, act upon the patient, but upon the magnetizer in enabling him to place himself in a special physical and moral state which induces him to act. This is, moreover, the opinion of Lafontaine, whose authority in practice cannot be contested.

I will cite a personal example demonstrating beyond question that magnetization does really consist in a communication of the magnetizer's own movement to the magnetized subject, and that will power is not present in this communication. It has happened to me that while I was in an excited state brought on by anger, a patient in an enfeebled condition has come to me for treatment. I felt strong, *vibrating*, capable of acting with great energy, and consequently of augmenting the organic functions of my patient. And during the seance, the patient, as a matter of fact, experienced much stronger effects than usual, but the next day he told me he would have been benefited by the treatment had he not felt all day angry and irritable, conditions unusual with him. My state of mind, which could not have been detected by any outward sign, had therefore been communicated against my own will, for it is clear I tried to hide it as much as possible.

A magnetizer, whether amateur or professional, must be strong, robust, complete master of himself, and as well balanced as possible from a physical and moral point of view; because an operator who is weak would not only weaken himself more by magnetizing but, as we can readily understand, he would have a tendency to communicate to the subject the disease which is the cause of his weakness or ill-health, for he could not transmit anything else than the action of his own sickly movement. But it should be well understood, especially in home circles, that in all instances where health is normal (which is the case with three-fourths of the human race) acute diseases can be avoided by taking measures in time. And even when a malady does break out, it can almost always be rendered mild where it might have been mortal. This is equivalent to saying that, with sufficient vigilance, we can cure all sicknesses. But as this vigilance is often lacking, an acute malady may end fatally, or pass on to a chronic state to become incurable. In this latter case it is again necessary to know that, to a very great extent, we may always, no matter how grave the case may be, relieve the patient and prolong his days, in making his existence bearable. Magnetism can thus cure or relieve all sickness. When this truth is known and understood, we shall no longer see one-half of humanity drag out a languishing life without the possibility of its burden being lightened. In the bosom of the family the father will be doctor to his wife, and she will be doctor to her husband and children. In obstinate or complicated cases recourse will be had to the physician or professional magnetizer, who will know how to bring about a cure, or at least, the wished-for betterment. I wish to say a few words more about the magnetizer. According to what has already been stated, we conceive that there exist individuals, highly gifted by nature, who soon become operators of exceptional ability, tact and dexterity, able to heal rapidly almost all cases; whereas many others less highly gifted, possessed of a more scientific, theoretical and practical training than the first category of persons just referred to, will not be able to obtain the same number of cures with the same ease. Therefore, among professionals there will always be strong and weak, good operators and mediocre operators. It will be the duty of such patients as are not magnetized at home in their family to be able to distinguish the one from the other.

CHAPTER IV.

PHYSICAL LAWS OF HUMAN MAGNETISM—POLARITY
OF THE BODY—RULES OF MAGNETIC ACTION—AP-
PLYING MAGNETISM IN CORRECT POSITIONS.

I have said that the magnetic agent is subject
to laws which can be reduced to exact formula.
I will not give here the scientific demonstration
of this assertion. It will suffice if I present a
few indications indispensable to those who will
only read this work, and if I set forth the general
laws of human magnetism.

The magnetic agent offers many points of
analogy with the other natural forces, heat, light,
electricity and more particularly with the magnetism proper to the lodestone. And the laws
which regulate the action of the magnetism of
the lodestone are those which regulate the force
of physiological magnetism, whatever may be
its origin. Moreover, in the time of Paracelsus,
when the hermetic philosophers established the
theory of the universal fluid, they recognized
(and so have all those who have succeeded
them) that the human body possesses properties
similar to those of the magnet, and that is the
reason they gave the name of *magnetism* to the
force of this property. Mesmer, who, almost
at the end of the 18th century, claims to be the
inventor of magnetism, tells us, "there are mani-

fested, particularly in the human body, properties analogous to those of the magnet. We can there equally distinguish poles divers and opposite which can be communicated, charged, destroyed or re-enforced; even the phenomenon of deviation is observed there. The property of the animal body manifested by its analogy with the magnet has led me to call it *animal magnetism."*

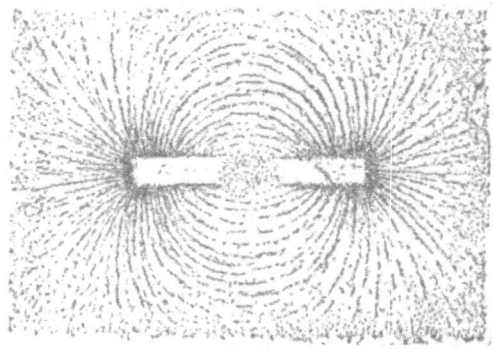

FANTOME MAGNÉTIQUE.

As has been recognized by Paracelsus, and after him Van Helmont, Robert Fludd, de Reichenbach, de Rochas and many others, the human body is polarized like a magnet, or rather, like an assemblage of magnets. It therefore has its neutral lines and its opposite poles. The poles are the axes around which circulate currents similar to those of the pile. They constitute likewise the principal starting points of the waves which transmit to the ether the vibratory movement of the various parts constituting the organism, which we may call, as I have said, the action of our movement. With this difference, that the human body does not attract fire in the ether, these waves, leaving each pole considered as principal center of expansion, behave in a manner which bears some resemblance to that shown by the magnetic phantom for the action of the magnet. The accompanying figure makes us understand very clearly how human magnetism is transmitted through space. I will only say here, without further explanation, that the principal axe divides the human body laterally from right to left; that the right side is positive, and the left negative. The poles are at the hands and feet, while the neutral line is at the top of the head. This is the lateral axe. Another axe of less importance separates the front from the back of the body, the front is positive, like the right side, the back (spine, nape of the neck) is negative like the left side. The poles are at the forehead and at the top of the neck, the neutral point is at the perineum. These two axes, which constitute the entire polarity, are represented by the cut, in which we see two interlocked horseshoe magnets. A secondary polarity exists, but as a knowledge of it is not essential for magnetizing, therefore to avoid lengthening out this descrip-

tion, I will not speak of it here. By using the
arithmetical signs X and —, employed in electrical science to designate the poles of the pile,
the entire polarity of the human body is thus
shown. To this distribution of the polarity of
the human body there are some exceptions: for
instance, in left-handed persons it is reversed.
In these persons the right side is always negative,
and the left side positive. In ambidextrous per-

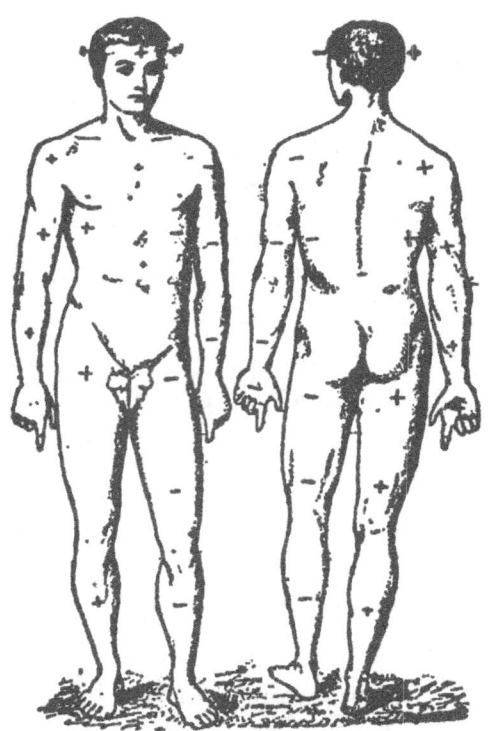

POLARITÉ D'ENSEMBLE DU CORPS HUMAIN.

sons, i. e., those who use both hands equally well for the same object, polarity is inconstant.

We know that in two bodies charged with the same electricity there is repulsion, whereas they attract each other when charged with opposite electricity. Two magnets repulse each other by their same poles, and are attracted to each other by their opposite poles. It is the same with the human body. Not only two individuals placed near each other, act one upon the other as I have stated before, but we see that standing, they are attracted toward each other or repulsed, according as they present their same or opposite poles to each other. An example will make this clear. The right hand (positive) presented to the forehead (positive) of subject repulses him, whereas the same hand (positive) attracts him at the nape of the neck (negative). Inversely, the left hand attracts at the forehead, and repulses at the nape of the neck. This phenomenon, which is quite perceptible in most individuals, is manifested with great intensity in sensitive persons, and soon causes an increase or decrease of organic activity which nearly always leads to contracture or paralysis. Bearing in mind the phenomenon of increase or decrease of organic activity under the action of the same or opposite poles or sides, we can readily understand that according to the manner of applying magnetism, we can *calm* or *excite.*

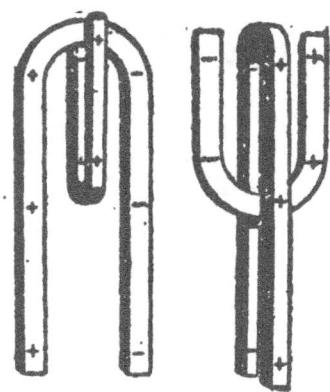

Taking this principle as a basis, I have reduced to three the number of general rules which regulate the action of human magnetism, and which I formulate as follows:

First law.—The human body is polarized; the right side is positive, the left, negative.

Second law.—Polarity is reversed in left-handed persons.

Third law.—The same poles excite, the opposite poles calm.

In the organism, the magnetic force may be considered as an equilibrating principle; but the equilibrium of the whole series of the organic functions, the reducing or restoring of this ensemble of functions to the normal pitch of the motion it ought to attain and not sensibly exceed if a good state of health is to be maintained, is all the more readily established in that we act more in conformity with the laws regulating its action. If the magnetizers of old (who only knew of one thing, viz., the *fluid*, transmitted haphazard, without method) were able to relieve the patients they magnetized, it is clear they would have been able to relieve them better and more rapidly if they had transmitted this so-called fluid, i. e., that form of our movement, in conforming to the laws governing its transmission. Referring the reader to the next chapter for the description of the practice of magnetism, I will only add here that the chief instrument of the magnetizer being his hands, in using them conformably to the laws of polarity, he can, at will, in a certain measure, calm or excite the ensemble of the organic functions; that is, he can bring them back to the normal action of their movement. In the first case, standing in front of the patient, it suffices to act with both hands in such a way that his right hand is directed toward the left side, and his left hand toward the right side, as shown by Figure I in the group herewith.

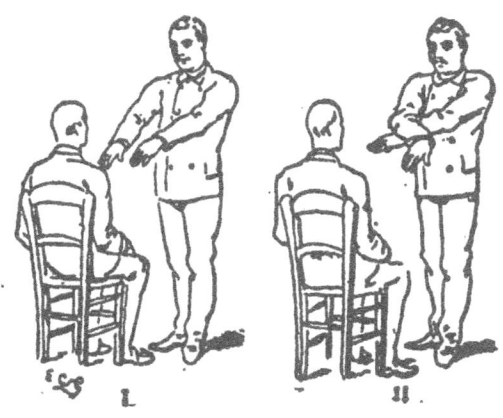

This is called the *heteronomic* action, from the Greek prefix *hetero,* meaning different. In the second case, standing in front of the patient, as before, you cross your hands, or better still, using one at a time, you apply your right hand to the right side, and your left hand to the left side, as indicated by figure II. This is the *isonomic* action, from the Greek prefix *iso,* signifying equal, same. Let me add a few more remarks for those who know the former theories or intend to study them.

Since the revival of magnetism, which took place at the beginning of the 16th century, almost all practitioners have attached very great importance to the part that will-power plays in the production of magnetic effects. Having shown that the action of the will is almost nothing (except for aiding the magnetizer to put himself into a special vibratory condition, an active state as distinguished from the passive state which the patient is in) I will not return to the subject again.

Under the action of magnetism practiced by an experienced operator, an immediate lowering of the patient's temperature and fever is visible, and the delirium of acute affections ceases as if by magic. The anaemic rapidly regains his strength, he who is wasted by a long series of suffering experiences, in a single seance, considerable comfort, enabling him to recover his sleep, appetite and lost strength. The dying are resurrected in a few hours, and, snatched from the brink of the grave, are spared, to give their full measure of the work to be accomplished here below. In a word, it appears that we transmit strength, health and life, or at least a part of the strength, health and life which we possess. And it is precisely the observation of these vital phenomena under magnetic action which, from Maxwell to Lafontaine, has compelled most magnetizers to suppose the magnetic fluid to be nothing else than our vital principle which is communicated to the patient. Notwithstanding appearances, such is not the case. To begin with, we cannot retain the vital principle any longer because the wave theory suppresses all the fluids except the ether, in order to allow only transformation of movement to subsist. Furthermore, if there existed within us a vital principle which we could consider as a natural force, the simplest reasoning would suffice to show that it would be entirely different from the magnetic force. For, if we find the magnetic force in the human body and in living organisms, we also find it present in these same bodies after life has abandoned them. Experiments I have made with the human skeleton and with organs and members of dead animals, at varying periods after death, clearly prove that the magnetic force is still there where the vital principle has disappeared. Magnetic force must not be considered otherwise than as a special property of matter which is manifested by a particular movement of the atoms of which it is composed.

If any doubt of this should still remain, it will disappear when you consider that, as I have pointed out, magnetic force is present not only in organic bodies living and dead, but is also seen in inorganic bodies, as likewise in all the forces or agents of nature.

Here is another observation which also has an important theoretical bearing. Some operators, and particularly certain medical magnetizers, supposed the magnetic fluid to be identical with what the physiologists of the period called the nervous fluid, and as far as their knowledge went, the two words were synonymous. This identity is comprehensible because they thought that magnetism acted specially on the nerves, that it was more efficacious in nervous than in organic affections, and that, while curing nervous disorders, such as hysteria and epilepsy, it could, in some cases, determine mesmeric sleep similar to symptomatic crises. Acting on the nerves, it was supposed to follow their length throughout the different parts of the body.

Now, in order to rectify this erroneous idea, I will only submit one argument. That there does exist in us a nervous force transmitting sensitive impressions from without to the brain, and motor impressions from the brain without, there is not any doubt, but this force, which is *no longer a fluid* but a special form of movement, is by no means the same as the magnetic force. I will prove it in a few words. The nerves cross each other in the depths of the cerebral mass in the corpus callosum in such a manner that those originating in the left hemisphere are distributed over the right side of the body; and inversely, those which originate in the right hemisphere go over to animate the left side. Now, it is evident that the road followed by the motor and sensory impressions, is that of the nerves themselves, just as telegraphic or telephonic transmission follows the length of the wires which connect one station with another. If the magnetic force were the nervous force it would follow, as does the nervous force, the length of the nerves, and the hemispheres of the brain would be of opposite polarity to their corresponding sides. But we know that such is not the case, and that all the right side from the sole of the foot to near the top of the head is positive, while the same parts on the opposite side are negative. After this outline of theory, which states and explains the purposes of human magnetism, I will proceed to describe the methods to be employed in magnetizing.

PART II.

CONTENTS.

PART II.

INTRODUCTION TO PART II.

As already pointed out in the preceding chapter, the action of our movement is communicated around us by successive waves, and the extent of these waves constitutes the field of our physical action. This field of action may be compared to the magnetic field of a magnet and to the hertian waves which serve as a basis for the demonstration of wireless telegraphy. While of much greater extent than the magnetic field, it is considerably smaller than the field of electrical waves.

When a debilitated patient is placed in the field of action of a healthy, cheerful, strong and robust individual, a communication, a vitalizing current is established between the strong man and his weak patient, and the equilibrium which constitutes health tends to set in in both, without their will power having any share in this action. It is for this reason that, in the ordinary relations of life, the weak seek out the protection of the strong, the child is so happy in its mother's arms, and that the patient worn out by long suffering, feels relief, calm and comfort in the presence of a sympathetic and strong friend. It is an *unconscious, involuntary magnetism*, the reality and

importance of which must be patent to everybody. Intention, desire, will power, especially
in the case of one dear to us, give greater impulsion to our magnetic radius, and an intenser current is directed toward the patient. The love of
a mother for the child which she presses to her
breast drives away many of its pains, relieves
others, and spares it from more than one grave
malady which might not always yield to even the
best prepared medicaments. This is *instinctive
magnetism*, possessing undoubted advantages
over involuntary magnetism. I will not go into
the theory of this more deeply, but to make its
true value apparent, I cite the two following examples which are recorded respectively by the
Marquis de Puysegur, in his *Researches Physiol-
ogiques Sur l'Homme*, p. 67; and by Dr. Foissac,
in his *Rapports et Discussions de l'Academie
Royale de Medecine Sur le Magnetisme Animal*,
p. 272.

First example. "The Princess de Ligne, *nee*
Pozzodi Borgo, who certainly had never heard of
Mesmer or his doctrine, had one of her children
in the cradle sick with small pox, and whose side
she had not quitted since the outbreak of the
malady. Being obliged to go out on important
business, she started at a time her child went to
sleep. Imagine her surprise and fright on returning home to find all her servants in tears.
They told her the doctor whom they had sum-

moned had not arrived. She questioned them further and they told her the child she had left sleeping peacefully woke up almost immediately, and after crying and complaining for some minutes, the pimples became so faint and flat that they could not hide from the mother the danger in which her child was. Without answering a single word, without uttering a cry, and paying attention only to the maternal instinct burning within her, Mme. de Ligne went to the cradle, took out her child, and in the transport of despair she put him on the ground, his body covered by hers and her clothing, and she remained over him for half an hour in a sort of trance and as if prostrated or in the depths of the darkest meditation. During that time, listening to and hearing nothing around her, no human force would have been capable of taking her away from the place where the attraction of her feelings held her magnetically fixed, till finally the child's cries reminding her of its existence, brought her out of her stupor. She got up and uncovered him, he breathed freely and his eyes opened again. From that moment the sickness followed its course, and the child soon recovered its health. This feeling, resulting from maternal love, which no resolution or reflection had prepared beforehand, is undoubtedly a phenomenon of instinctive animal magnetism."

Second example "Among the cures operated

by M. Desprez, there is one which it is important to remember, viz., that of his wife. She experienced, after a confinement, very serious accidents against which all help for the time being was unsuccessful. The patient lost her strength, and, feeling her end approaching, addressed a last good-bye to her husband, and fell back apparently quite dead. His confreres (Mr. Desprez was a doctor) and his friends, thinking her dead, wanted to force Mr. Desprez from the room, but, riveted there by hope against hope, he refused to leave, and begged to be left alone with her. After all had left the room, he hastily closed the door, undressed himself, went to bed next to his wife, took her in his arms, tried to warm her and bring her back to life. At the end of twenty minutes she heaved a deep sigh, opened her eyes, recognized him, and recovered her speech! A few days later she was restored to health."

If our life, our strength and our energy can be communicated from the strong to the weak without the will-power of either taking part consciously in this communication, it is evident that under the influence of a design thoroughly determined upon, of an ardent desire, of a powerful will, much more satisfactory results will be obtained by proceeding according to the rules of the art, for then we can regulate our action and bring it to bear upon any desired organ, either to soothe or to excite. The magnetic force escapes from all parts of the body and radiates around us in modifying (were I a believer in the fluid theory, I would say in saturating) everything which environs us. But certain parts of the body give out more than others. The three principal sources are: The extremities, that is, the *hands,* especially the palm and fingers; the *eyes*—the gaze, and the *lungs*—breath.

There are two kinds of magnetization which can be practiced independently of each other, or, what is preferable, they may be combined: *direct magnetization* and *indirect* or *intermediate magnetization.*

The first kind is operated directly upon the patient; and the second by means of liquids, food or objects magnetized beforehand, and which are to be absorbed or worn by the patient. I will describe first the ordinary methods of direct magnetization.

In the ordinary relations of life, the hands are for man the organ of prehension par excellence. In magnetism they become the poles; that is to say, the principal centers whence start out the waves which carry without us the action of our movement. They also serve largely to direct the magnetic agent, i. e., the waves constituted by the action of our movement, towards the organ or portion of the body that thought has indicated in advance.

Healers of all ages, from the greatest miracle-workers to the commonest quacks, have used the hand as the principal vehicle of their action. That is why Homer says in the *Iliad* that certain men have a *medical hand,* meaning by that a hand which seemed to possess of itself the property or virtue of healing diseases. This virtue was often limited to distinct maladies, or rather, what appears to me most probable, the operator restricted in this manner, without being aware of it, the extent of his power. Thus Pyrrhus, king of Epirus, cured the disorders of the liver, in touching the region of the organ, not with his hand, but with his foot; another arrested burns, while sores, fever, scrofula, etc., were cured by as many others; and all, or nearly all, pretended to have this power as a gift from heaven.

J. B. Thiers relates that certain families had the privilege of curing ganglion by touching; others, excrescences, etc. Only a member of the family of Saint Catherine, and born in March or April, could have the gift of these cures. (Des Superstitions 1, 6 p. 518.)

This manner of healing diseases by using the hand was generally called the *touch* or *touching.*

With some doctors or clever non-mystical healers the touching consisted of a series of fairly accurate but complicated manipulations, such as stroking, feeling or handling, pressing, rubbing, etc., but the mystics only touched while making invocations. Jesus, Apollonius of Thyane, Simon the magician, the emperors Vespasian and Adrian have all operated cures, some of them instantaneous, by a simple touching of the hand, or in making movements similar to those of the methods we employ at this day. The Kings of France, from Clovis to Louis XV, touched the sick after the coronation ceremony, and healed great numbers. Art has bequeathed to us numerous works in which we can clearly see the thought of the artist has been to consider the hand as the instrument of healing. The word *touching* was so frequently employed to designate the various operations practiced by the hand, that Mesmer and Puysegur constantly use it synonymously for *to magnetize*.

At the present day magnetization by the hands comprises a series of rational and methodical manipulations, the efficacy of which is proved by the experience of three centuries. The number of these manipulations may be reduced to five principal groups. They are: *Passes, Imposition, Application, Stroking, Rubbing.*

CHAPTER I.

THE MAGNETIC PASS—LONGITUDINAL PASS—FIRST, SECOND, AND THIRD POSITIONS — TRANSVERSAL PASS—CORRECT POSITION.

The magnetic process which we employ today under the name of *passes* does not appear to have been used under this name by the celebrated healers of antiquity. They practiced what was then called the *laying on of the hands,* which seems to comprise the action of the hand immobile presented at a distance (our imposition of today) and the action of the hand likewise presented at a distance but in movement (pass). Such at least is what we are able to gather from the examination of art records which succeeding generations have left us.

I here reproduce three figures in which it will be clearly seen, and especially in the third, that the hand, or the hands execute movements at a distance, and in a downward direction, that is, passes as we execute them today. Passes executed either with one or both hands, are *longitudinal* or *transversal.*

Longitudinal Passes.—Practice. Longitudinal passes are executed either only on the part affected, on one side of the body or on both sides at the same time; from the top of the head to the lower part of the trunk, and even from the head to the extremity of the feet, and always in a downward, never in an upward, direction.

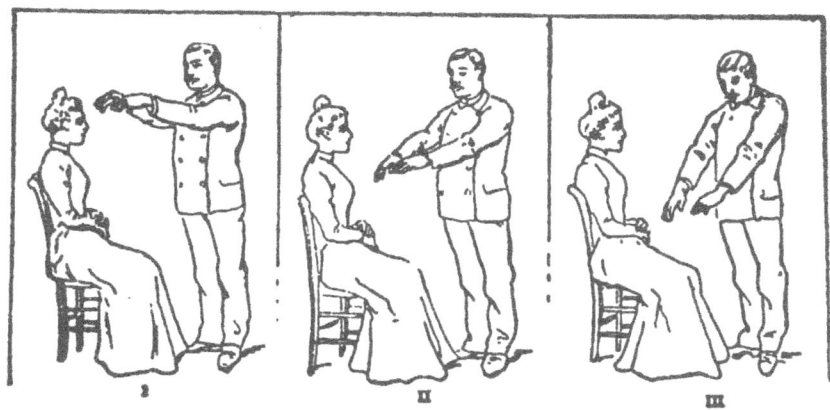

A longitudinal pass, taking as an example a pass executed from the head to the lower part of the trunk, is generally practiced in the following manner:

You begin on the top of the head and go down the length of the trunk. Do not use any muscular strength. Expose, but do not tender your hand, keep it stretched out, the fingers slightly, but not widely separated from each other. Your hand must be in a flat position, the palm undermost, and as if held up in the air; then you let it go down, as if you were going to draw with your fingers five perpendicular lines on the surface of the body, or better still, as if you were going to distribute in a downward direction—*a something,* no matter what, let us say the magnetic force—which you are supposed to have poured on the head and chest. The moment your hands reach the limit of their downward course, you close them as if to hold for a second the magnetic force which continues to escape. You then bring your hands above the head, being careful to lift them up, not opposite the body, as that might trouble the movement imparted by the preceding pass, but sideways. When your closed hands have reached the top of the head you open them in extending the fingers slightly as if to pour or spread about your handful of *something* (in order to materialize the thought let us say a handful of bran) and then you bring them slowly down again, as I have just said.

That was the manner in which most of the old magnetizers practised longitudinal passes.

Starting from the principle that on an organ you often execute passes with a single hand, and that it is awkward to lift it up sideways, in describing an ellipsis, instead of lifting up my hands on the right and left of the patient, I prefer to draw the upper part of my body back, so as to separate myself from the patient, and to raise my hands a little above the level of the top of the head, in passing them with fists closed in front of my chest. These two groups of figures show the various movements of a pass, which I divide into two *grades*: in the first *grade* I execute a pass; in the second *grade,* I prepare to execute another. In the first grade represented by the figures of the first group, I act as if I were pouring out the magnetic force on the patient at the height of his or her forehead (Fig. 1); then I bring my hands down the sides or the front of the body (Fig. 2); and, continuing their course my hands reach the lower part of the trunk (Fig. 3). At that stage, the first grade is executed, and properly speaking, the first pass is done. But I have to prepare myself to execute another. For that, as the figures of the second group show, I close my hands in drawing them toward myself (Fig. 4); then, drawing back my body so as to separate myself from the patient, and bringing my elbows near my body, I raise my closed hands, their outside facing the patient (Fig. 5); and lift them about 3 or 4 inches above my head (Fig. 6). Then, being ready to execute a second pass, I have only to turn my hands the palm toward the patient, and to *pour out* the magnetic force (or, as the old magnetizers called it, the *fluid*) on the frontal region (Fig. 7), and continue in the same way.

Practiced very slowly, at a distance of 2 to 4 inches, longitudinal passes *charge, saturate* the body of the subject, and their action usually results in a feeling of calm and comfort. A longitudinal pass executed very slowly takes at least

30 seconds. Executed a little faster, at a distance of 6 to 12 inches, they become stimulating and

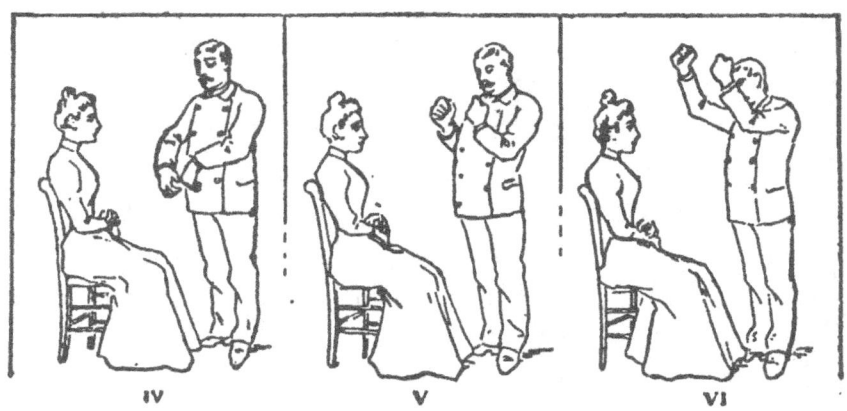

IV   V   VI

their action is almost always perceptible in the form of a mild current which, in the interior of the body, follows and even precedes the motion made by the hand of the magnetizer. Practiced rapidly, in a downward direction at a distance of from 12 to 16 inches, they take the name of *long passes*. Their action, which is likewise stimulating, clears the head and chest, warms the extremities, carries off the humors and regulates the circulation. Under the action of passes practised very slowly, first from the head to the stomach, and then on the head only, sensitive subjects fall into the magnetic sleep.

It sometimes happens that sensitive subjects, and likewise nervous patients who are magnetized for the first time, experience a feeling of oppression which might even lead to suffocation. This little feeling of discomfort is avoided by making long passes from the head to the feet, or, better still, by making transversal passes on the head and chest.

Transversal Passes. How to practice them.

Transversal passes have the opposite effect of longitudinal passes practiced very slowly. I might almost say that if the action of the latter is magnetizing, the action of the former is de-magnetizing. For they clear and lighten the heavy and congested head, arrest all sensation of oppression, wake up the somnambule put to sleep magnetically, and always leave a feeling of calm and comfort accompanied by an agreeable glow.

The transversal, like the longitudinal, pass is executed in two grades; in the *first grade* you execute the pass, in the *second grade,* you prepare yourself to execute another.

In the first grade, represented by the four figures of our illustration, you see the position of the arms, forearms and hands. In Fig. 1 the forearms are crossed at about the middle of the chest, the hands are quite wide open, their palms facing the patient, the thumbs down, and the fingers slightly apart without being stretched out. Fig. 2.—The arms are spread out somewhat, and the hands with the forearms commence to execute a movement of rotation which will turn the

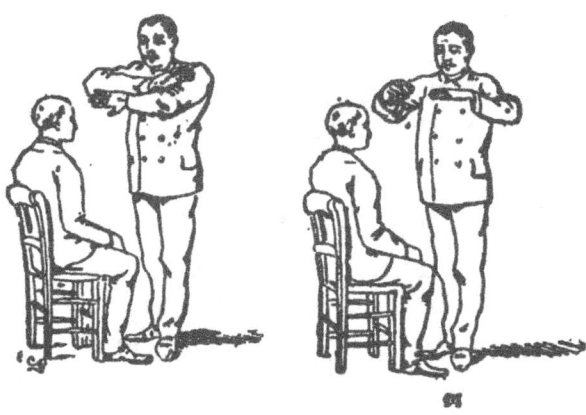

hand in such a manner that, the arms being open, the palms remain directed toward the patient, with the thumbs up. Fig. 3.—The arms are stretched out, the hands and forearms turn, and

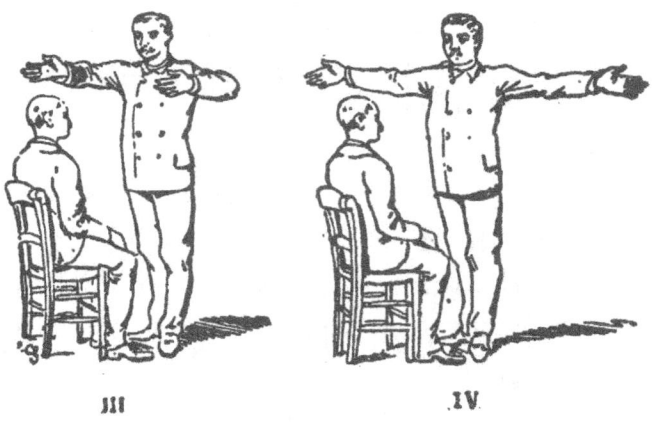

the movement which has been started, is continued. Fig. 4.—The arms are stretched out wide and form a horizontal line, the palm of the

hands faces the patient, and the fingers are still slightly separated from each other without being stretched out.

Second grade. The arms being in the position indicated by Fig. 4, the forearms have only to be brought in front of each other by turning the hands, in order to return to the position of Fig. 1 and to continue rapidly, in successively spreading out and crossing the arms, as if to fan the patient and agitate the air around him.

Transversal passes are mostly practiced above the head, and on the face and chest, but they can also be practiced on the sides, the spine and the legs. Their action is calmative, influencing all the parts of the body.

The magnetizers of former times employed transversal passes a great deal to loosen the sick, or at least, the parts affected. With the theory of emission, the use of this method was justified, because it was believed that a fluid of bad quality enveloped the patient or the parts affected, and that it was imperative to get rid of it. Magnetizers of the present day do not loosen their patients so much, and they are right. As a matter of fact, this loosening does not seem to me to be very useful, except when the patient is dull, or when his head is heavy, hot or congested.

CHAPTER II.

Imposition—Laying on of Hands—Historical Facts
—Palmar Imposition—Rotary Imposition—Digital Imposition—Perforating Imposition—How
to Practice the Movements.

The imposition of the hands on the patient is one of the most powerful processes of contemporary magnetism. With the ancients, it constituted the basis of what we might call today *occult or divine magnetism.* It is especially by the *laying on of the hands* that the priests and persons·initiated in the mysteries of religion in Egypt, worked those wonderful cures of which history has handed down to us the account. The historic wood cut, by an unknown artist, represents a seated figure, evidently possessed of great moral authority, pointing his left hand, armed with a wand, toward a subject who appears to have fallen into a fit, appeals to me as the most complete demonstration of the practice of magnetism by the Egyptians, by the process which we call today the *laying on of the hands,* or, *imposition.* Another, and no less curious figure, can be seen at the Bibliotheque Nationale. It is a scene from the zodiac of Deuderah representing the great Egyptian goddess magnetizing her son Orus, whom she holds standing up in her left hand, by imposing her right hand toward him.

I say "magnetizing her son," because that is the interpretation given by Deleuze, and to my knowledge no other satisfactory explanation has been given either before or since.

With the Hebrews, the laying on of the hands was employed on many occasions, not only by the prophets and the various healers for healing the sick, but also for the purpose of transmitting any power from one person to another. On the death-bed, the blessing which was to attract to the head of him who received it the favor of the Eternal was given by the imposition of the hands. The gift of prophecy was often communicated in the same way, not only by men, but by the Eternal, "God laid His hands upon him and he prophesied."

If God employed the laying on of hands toward man, it follows that men must have employed it among themselves. And we find very numerous proofs in all the books of the Old Testament that they did employ it. I will go even further than this and say that they always employed it.

When Moses designated Joshua to conduct the people of Israel to the promised land, he laid his hands upon him. "And Joshua, the son of Nun, was full of the spirit of wisdom; for Moses had laid his hands on him; and the children of Israel obeyed him, and did as the Lord commanded Moses." (Deut. 34.) In the war which Moses made with the Amalekites, it was seen that when, facing the enemy, he lifted up his hands to heaven, his army was victorious, but when he was tired, and he let his arms fall, the enemy, taking fresh courage, had the advantage. There is extant a rare engraving by Golthius which represents the lawgiver of the Hebrews in the act of laying on his hands in a manner similar to that which we use today for transmitting to our patients the action of our movement.

Pious souls instinctively raise their hands to heaven (a form of imposition) when they are in need of help and consolation. On such occasions, they do not give, but receive, for they are in a passive state, their souls are humbled.

According to the theory I have expounded in the preceding chapter, we can understand that, of themselves, and without any supernatural intervention, an equilibrium tends to set in between them and the aerial medium, and that a decided improvement must be the result.

Jesus, whom we see at the age of twelve years disputing among the doctors, disappeared from the scene of the world, to reappear toward his thirtieth year, which is the epoch when his mission became clearly defined. What did he do during this absence? Nobody knows, but it is exceedingly probable that, according to the custom of the sages of that remote period, he went to seek initiation in the temples of India, Greece or Egypt. In any case, he stored up knowledge, and then was revealed as the greatest worker of miracles known in history. How did he heal the sick who flocked to him? Often by touching, but oftener by the imposition of the hands. The text of the Gospels alone (leaving aside other historical works) proves this abundantly.

"Now when the sun was setting, all they that had any sick with divers diseases brought them unto him; and he laid his hands on every one of them, and healed them." (S. Luke iv., 40) "And he touched her hand and the fever left her." "And he cast out the spirits with his word and healed all that were sick." (S. Matth. viii., 15, 16.)

Jesus declares that the power of working miracles will belong to all those who have faith in him. "He that believeth and is baptized shall be saved." The miracles which accompany those who shall believe are that "they shall cast out devils in my name, they shall lay hands on the sick, and the sick shall recover." (S. Mark xvi., 16 to 18.)

The apostles continue to heal the sick by laying on the hands, and to work wonders. The early Christians held their belongings in common. Ananias and Sapphira, his wife, selling their possessions, kept back for themselves part of the proceeds of the sale, and brought the other part to Peter. Knowing what had occurred, Peter, holding out his hand toward Ananias, reproached him with what he had done, and Ananias fell down as if thunderstruck (Acts v.). The foregoing argument shows us the mechanism of this action, and enables us to understand how Peter's displeasure, transmitted by the imposition of his hand, was sufficient to convulse the subject by producing such a shock as to result in death.

Saint Paul was perhaps the apostle Jesus employed most in laying on of the hands for healing the sick. Being at Malta, where he stayed at the house of a man whose name was Melitus, and finding the father of this man lay sick of fever and dysentery, "Paul went to see him, prayed and laid his hands on him and healed him." (Acts xviii.)

After the times of the apostles the early church, and later, the exorcists, long employed the imposition of the hands for healing, and at the epoch when peoples' bodies were possessed of demons, for expelling these foul fiends and unclean spirits. Our churches and museums contain a great number of works of art in which the laying on of the hands occupies considerable space.

In imposition practiced by former magnetizers, the pictures showing this process, represent graphically the "magnetic fluid" issuing from the tips of the fingers, by dotted lines, giving an exact idea of its mode of communication. Imposition is divided into *palmar imposition* and *digital imposition.*

Palmar imposition. How to Practice it. Palmar imposition is practiced by presenting the palm of the hand at a distance of about 2 to 4 or even 8 inches from the part we wish to act upon, and in holding it in that position for a time varying from 1 to 5 minutes. This imposition is usually done with one hand only, as shown in the figure herewith, but it can be done with both

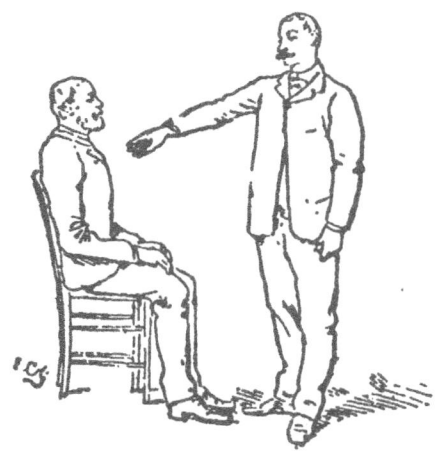

hands at the same time. It exerts a slightly stimulating effect when practiced in a heteronomous position, i. e., when the left hand is directed toward the right side, and the right toward the left side.

Digital imposition. How to practice it. Digital imposition is usually executed with the right hand, the fingers extended, firm, slightly separated from each other and directed during the same time at a distance of from 4 to 6 inches toward the parts you wish to act upon, as the figure herewith shows.

Rotary imposition. How to practice it. If a more powerful effect than the preceding be needed, the hand and the fingers being in the same position, you gently describe a concentric circle on or around the organ or the part it is desired to act upon, taking care that the motion of the hand is guided from left to right, i. e., in the same direction as the hands of a watch move. In this manner, the action of the movement works in agreement with the human magnetism, transmitted by the hand, and the action of the latter is considerably augmented. This process is termed rotary imposition.

Perforating imposition. How to practice it. If the fingers, being in the same position, and still slightly apart, but instead of executing rotary motions are turned and twisted around as if to perforate or bore a hole, the action becomes still more exciting. This process, which I call perforating imposition, is somewhat difficult to practice, and still more difficult for a teacher to explain if he does not combine practice with theory.

Under the action of rotary and particularly of perforation imposition, the patient soon perceives within him a motion similar to that executed near him by the hand of the operator. This movement, almost always accompanied by warmth, considerably augments the circulation and the secretions, separates and draws out stagnant humors and dissolves congestions in determining at first a phenomenon almost similar to that produced in an impure liquid when agitated with a stick. The right hand imposed on the forehead of a sensitive subject, standing up, renders his head heavy, produces warmth and brings on a sort of discomfort accompanied by aversion. The left hand imposed on the same part produces contrary effects. Whether the imposition is palmar or digital in leaving your hand in place without moving it, the first suffices to induce sleep in a very sensitive subject, the second to wake him up.

Imposition is generally employed on a patient to stimulate the functions and in such a case it is good to practice it in the isonomous position. Digital imposition exerts a more energetic influence than palmar imposition, rotary imposition is still more powerful, and the maximum of action is obtained by the use of perforating imposition combined with hot insufflation; this last process furnishes the magnetizer with the greatest amount of power he could wish for. Therefore the first method must be employed in all cases where it is required to slightly stimulate or regulate one or more functions of the body, and the second where it is necessary to excite them. Rotary and perforating imposition must be reserved for the treatment of obstinate constipation, congestion, obstruction, tumors and for certain cases of extreme debility. The augmented arterial action resulting from the use of this last method being considerable, it is necessary to point out, that it must not be used on starting treatment of a patient unless he is only slightly nervous and impressionable, because, particularly with hysterical persons, convulsions might ensue, and these are unnecessary and confusing for a practitioner at his first attempts.

CHAPTER III.

APPLICATION OF MAGNETISM IN HEALING—EXAMPLES
—CURING CONGESTED HEAD.

In his work *Medicina Aegyptiorum*, Prosper Alpini states that certain Egyptian women healed dysentery by placing their hand flat on the patient's navel. A papyrus recently discovered by Ebers in the ruins of Thebes contains this formula: "Place thy hands on him to soothe his pain, and say: let the pain disappear," confirms the use of the application of the hands by the Egyptians, in the treatment of disease. In the *Histoire du Ceil,* Vol. I, Pluehe publishes a very curious figure (plate XI) which he calls *the awakening of Orus.* On a bed, represented by the body of a lion, a child, Orus, is seen all swathed up, apparently asleep. Near him, Anubis applies his left hand to the child's chest, raising the right hand toward Isis standing at the head of the bed, as if to implore his aid. This figure plainly shows us an application of the hand which we might call today a magnetic application.

From a bas-relief also we learn that the application of the hands was employed by the healers of Greece. Standing up, a young man is seen, with his head inclined and bearing the expression of sad discomfort; a seated figure is laying her right hand on the patient's left temple, while her left hand is applied to the abdomen, clearly for the object of relieving him. Pliny, in book 7 of his *Natural History*, expresses himself as follows concerning the application of the hands practiced by certain persons: "Crates of Pergamus has written that there was in the Hellespont, not far from Parion, a particular class of men called ophiogenes, who possessed the gift of healing by touch the bite of serpents, and of extracting all the venom from the body by only applying their hands to it." Throughout all periods of history we find examples of the action of the hands applied to the sick. Here is one all the more curious because neither the one who relates it, nor the operator, could have known anything about magnetism, and because in any case, the apparent object was not to heal.

"Being extremely ill," says Mme. Guyon in her *Memoires*, "they sent for Father Lacombe to confess me. As soon as he entered the house my pains subsided, and after he had blessed me, in my room, by laying his hands on my head, I was absolutely well enough to go to mass. The doctors were so astonished at it that they did not know to what to attribute my recovery, because, being protestants, they were not inclined to think it a miracle." (Charpignon, Physiologie med et metaph du Mag. 1848, p. 153.) In the 17th century an Irish knight of the name of

Valentine Greatrakes acquired considerable fame in healing sicknesses by *touch* (as it was then called). The annexed illustration, copied from a book of the period, shows us that touching is practiced in the form of *the application of the hands.* The patient appears to be suffering from

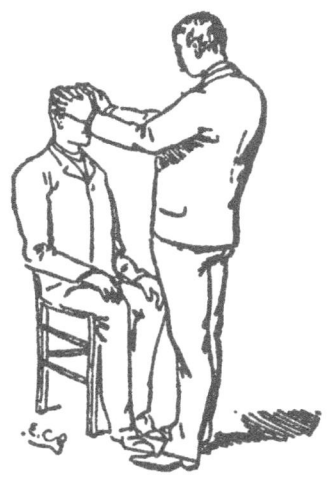

violent toothache, and, to calm it, the healer is applying his hands in a heteronomous position to the sides of the face. The figure, doubtless drawn from nature, may serve as a model for all those cases where application of the hands has to be made on the face with the object of calming.

In Turkey, where the practice of medicine is free to all without a license, the application of the hands in healing sicknesses is very general everywhere.

From *Therapeutique Magnetique,* another of
Du Potet's works, we copy the figure showing the
application of the fingers in an isonomous position practiced on the external orifice of the ears
with the object of curing deafness.

How to practice the application of the hands:
As you will have been able to judge from what
has been said, the art of making applications consists in placing or applying the hands flat on the
parts to be worked upon and to maintain them
there for a greater or shorter length of time. I
say the hands, because they are used oftenest,
but when it is necessary to work the region of the
back and the lower part of the spinal cord, there
is advantage in using the knees and also the sole
of the feet. Seated in front of the patient, applying your hands to his chest, you set the knees
against his knees and the feet against his feet.
You also place one or more fingers on the nerve
centers of the brain and spinal cord, on the eyes,
ears and on whichever part of the body you wish
to concentrate your action.

For headache brought on by a congestive state,
the operator, placed at the left of his patient, had
best apply the palm of his hands to the forehead
and back of the neck, the fingers slightly apart,
and pointed to the air instead of being flat on
the top of the head. In this case it would appear
that the surcharge of the head escapes at the tips

of the fingers, just as static electricity does by the ends. And indeed the operator clearly perceives a sensation of glow which, in the form of a current, escapes from the extremity of each finger, and the patient's head is gradually relieved.

As a calmative the applications are made as much as possible in a heteronomous position, whereas for exciting, it is preferable to practice them in the isonomous position. Their action is gentle and sound and they generally bring on after a few moments, a sensation of warmth all the more pleasant that the hands are cooler, particularly when the malady is of an inflammatory nature. In such instances it is advisable to plunge your hands into cold water frequently, so as to remove any unpleasant warmth communicated by the patient.

The practice of applications is suitable for all cases. Employed by itself it removes neuralgia and calms nearly every acute pain. Beginners especially should use them for a few seconds at the start of a sitting so as to establish (as Deleuze and Lafontaine have both pointed out) without any sudden transition, the rapport started between the magnetizer and the magnetized. The action of application being very mild, you avoid, in sensitive subjects, the attacks of convulsions which are always disagreeable, and often as discouraging for operators who are beginners as for the patients.

CHAPTER IV,

STROKING—POINTS OF DIFFERENCE FROM MASSAGE— HOW TO PERFORM STROKING.

Stroking consists of a slight touching repeated several times on the part it is desired to bring into action. It is in a measure a series of *applications in motion* or *longitudinal passes practiced with contact.* Stroking is borrowed from the usual methods of everyday massage, but with this difference that the magnetizer does not stroke in the same manner as the masseur. To begin with, the masseur operates directly on the patient's nude body, whereas the magnetizer strokes upon the clothes. The masseur with his strong manipulations, has for his particular object the acting mechanically on the circulation which drives the blood back to the heart. In order to do this he must exert a certain amount of pressure, starting at the extremities to arrive at the head, considered as the center. The action of the magnetizer, at a distance or by slight contact, has direct influence not on the circulation, but on the nervous system, which governs all the functions of the body, and his experience shows him that its action is specially felt on the motor nerves which lead from the brain, considered as the center, to the extremities. On account of the indisputable principles, for the masseur as well as for the magnetizer, the latter's stroking should always be downward, and the masseur's stroking is always upward.

And here I would offer a few words of important advice to young operators. They should, as much in the interest of their patients, as in order to establish their own personal theory, not only attentively study the effects of the various processes comparatively with each other, but vary the execution of each one of them. Now, for stroking which, practiced sometimes in an upward, sometimes in a downward, direction, the young operator will find that his patients will be unanimous in declaring that the first mode of execution is rather disagreeable to them, while the second is always agreeable. And inasmuch as an unpleasant sensation felt by a patient under the action of any manipulation is never of any use to him from a curative point of view, only such methods as are agreeable, and leave him after the seance, in a good physical and moral impression, should be employed.

Stroking, especially when practiced toward the end of the seance, regulates the magnetic action, clears the head, eases difficulty in breathing, and tends to warm cold hands and feet.

How to practice stroking. It is practiced on the greatest number of surfaces by applying the hands flat, the fingers slightly apart, and in bringing them down again from the upper to the lower part of the body, without any appreciable pressure. If you want to stroke the entire body, you do it in two movements, first from the head to the waist, then from the chest to the extremities. Standing up, and your patient sitting, you can work on him with both hands, and the process may be divided into two grades. *First grade.* Apply both your hands to the temples, and thumbs directed vertically toward the middle of the forehead, being about an inch or an inch and a half apart, while the fingers, slightly apart, rest upon the auricles as shown in the figure. *Second grade.* In taking care to curve in your hands to enable them to pass over the pavilions of the ears and yet stroking the sides of the throat, shoulders and forearms as far as the tips of the fingers. Replacing your hands in their position of the first grade, you go down the neck in following the direction of the sterno-cleido-mastoid muscle, then on the front of the chest as far as the waist. After repeating this operation five or six times, you sit down in front of your patient, and applying your hands to his chest you bring them down to the extremities, omitting the stomach, intestine, the thighs and legs. In order to practice stroking everywhere or over almost all parts, you again apply your hands to the lateral parts of the chest and bring them down to the extremities in passing (on the right) over the region of the liver, and (on the left) over that of the spleen, over the back, the hypochondrium, the external sides of the thighs and the legs. When the patient is in bed the stroking is practiced in a similar manner.

CHAPTER V.

RUBBING—DRY AND MOIST—HOW TO PRACTICE RUBBING—SLOW RUBBING—ROTARY RUBBING.

Rubbing is a strong or weak friction exercised upon a part of or the entire body, either with the hand alone or with a brush, glove or cotton cloth. It is also the action of passing the hands on the body, parts of the body, or in exercising a delicate pressure, a sort of gentle massage. Rubbing is said to be *dry* when it is practiced with the hand only, or with instruments only; it is said to be *moist* when there is added any liquid or semi-liquid substance, (grease, oil, alcohol, vinegar, etc.) either pure or medicated. Magnetic rubbing is always dry and practiced with the hand only; in massage it is sometimes moist, and is likewise practiced with the hand alone.

Rubbing produces a stimulating effect on the peripheric innervation. The circulation is accelerated, the blood flowing quickly through the veins gives increased color and warmth; and finally nutriment is assimilated in normal condition. This excitation, limited at first to the functions of the skin, is transmitted to the subcutaneous tissues, then to the veins, muscles, nerves, and to the deepest organs. We instinctively apply it to ourselves to combat the feeling of cold on the uncovered parts of the body, and especially on the hands, to lessen the painful sensation produced by a blow, or a fall, etc. This shows its use dates from the remotest antiquity.

Prosper Alpini tells us in *De Medicinae Egyptiorum* that medical and mysterious rubbings were the secret remedies used by the Egyptian priests for healing incurable diseases. Hippocrates wrote a treatise on frictions which has not come down to us, but he refers to it in his "Treatise on Articulations" in the following words: "A doctor ought to know many things; he should not be unacquainted with the benefits to be derived from rubbing. With its application quite contrary effects may be produced; it loosens stiff joints and gives tone and strength to those which are relaxed." Celsus, one of the great physicians at the beginning of the Christian era, was an ardent partisan of the practice. In his works published in French under the title of *Traduction des ouvrages de Aurelius Cornelius Celse, sur la medicine,* he gives a detailed account of massage and enumerates the chief diseases which can be cured or relieved by this method. After criticising Asclepiades' book, in which the author declares himself in favor of frictions, Celsus tells us that its use had been long known, and that what Asclepiades writes about it had all been written before by previous physicians. Thus, Hippocrates is said to have written, that violent friction hardens and delicate friction softens the tissues; that long continued friction emaciates, and when of short duration it produces corpulence. "Then," Celsus continues, "if we wish to consider all these kinds of rubbing, which, however, do not at all come within the province of medicine, we shall see that they all proceed from the same cause, which consists of suppression. For you do not bind up a thing but in removing that which rendered it lax, you only soften another in carrying off that which caused the hardness; we get stout, not by rubbing, but by the nourishment penetrating to the skin, which has been previously loosened by friction. The cause of these different effects depends, therefore, only on the manner of operating the rubbing; it is necessary to use emollients and to rub the body gently in acute diseases, even in their incipience, provided there is diminution in intensity of the fever, and before meals; on the other hand, there is danger in using strong rubbing in grave maladies where the patient gets worse (unless in cases of pleurisy) when you wish to procure sleep for patients. Therefore, rubbing should only be employed in maladies of long standing and which begin to decrease. It is as dangerous to use rubbing in the paroxysm of fever as it is useful to use it where the malady begins to diminish. We should even wait as long as possible, till the fever has disappeared, or at least, till it has lost its intensity. Rubbing is operated sometimes over all parts of the body, as when we wish to induce embonpoint in a slim person; sometimes only locally, when the weakness of that part requires it. Rubbing calms headaches of long standing, provided, however, the manipulation is not done during violent pain. It sometimes happens, also, that rubbing restores a paralyzed member. It is usual, however, to practice the rubbing on the parts that are not infirm. Friction on the lower parts, for instance, after relieving the middle or upper part of the body. Some manipulators are desirous of fixing the number of rubbings to be made on a person. But they are wrong, because this depends entirely upon the strength of the subject needing them. Fifty rubbings on a weak   subject are enough, whereas a strong man could stand two hundred, in proportion to the strength of operator and subject. Thus, we give fewer to a woman than to a man, fewer to a child or an old man than to a young man; finally, if you rub only certain parts, the rubbing should be hard and last some time, since it is impossible to enfeeble the body quickly by only rubbing one portion of it, and that it is necessary to drive away much matter, whether you want to clear the thin part you are rubbing or any other part; but if the weakness of the entire body requires that the rubbing be used equally all over it, it ought to last less time and be more gentle, so that it suffices to soften only the surface of the skin in order for it to be in a condition to receive the new matter which will be furnished to it by food to be taken immediately after the rubbings. We have already mentioned that the patient was in great danger when he was thirsty and burning inside, while the outside of his body remained cold. The only help in such a case is rubbing; if it brings warmth to the body externally the patient can recover."

In Rome at the time of Celsus (1st century) all classes of society employed frictions; those who were in good health went to be rubbed to maintain their health, and those who were ill were rubbed to recover it. The athletes were rubbed all over their body, so as to be more agile, and old people in order to get strength. From Rome the use of rubbing (to which were added emollients and some of the manipulations of massage as we have it today) soon spread all over the Orient, where it has been preserved to the present day. Alexander of Tralles, a celebrated Greek physician of the sixth century, and one of the last of those initiated into the mysteries of the pious ancients, often employed rubbing. Following the example of Celsus, he teaches that, practiced on the lower members, rubbing throws off morbid matters, calms the nervous system and facilitates perspiration. It calms convulsions, and acts powerfully against dropsy, because it opens the pores, lessens and divides the humors. In crises of epilepsy he executed moderate friction longitudinally on the members; then he felt and gently touched the eyes. He makes mention of the efficacy of the secret frictions of the Egyptian priests, and specially points out two characteristics that most magnetizers of today still consider indispensable in producing magnetic power, namely, great confidence on the part of the subject, and strong will power on the part of the physician. He affirms that it was to these secret rubbings Hippocrates alluded when he said that such things ought to be shown to sacred persons and not to the profane. If we are to believe Pe-

ter Borel, a learned historian who was physician
to Louis XIII., rubbing was even used to cure
fever. "A man named Degoust," he says, "clerk
of the court at Nismes, healed and does heal
every day a multitude of persons sick with the
fever only by rubbing their arms, and he found
out he possessed this gift by observing that all
the persons whose arms he rubbed got better
when he attached amulets around their wrists,
and when he discontinued attaching amulets the
people continued to heal just the same, by the
rubbing only." In northern countries, when
freezing threatens the parts of the body exposed
to the air, especially the nose and ears, dry rubbing is applied to quicken the circulation of the
blood, and if frozen, the part is rubbed with snow
or iced water. In syncope, after having taken off
the clothes covering the chest, some physicians
recommend the use of rubbing on the praecordia,
and the method has a certain amount of efficacy.
In reviving the bodies of new born children in a
state of apparent death, dry or moist rubbings
are used (moist with wine, vinegar, alcohol, etc.)
on the chest, back, the soles of the feet and the
palms of the hands. In the treatment of the apparently drowned, in most cases of paralysis, diminished circulation, general debility, violent
pains, acute rheumatism, etc., rubbing with emollients is effective. Rubbing has, therefore, con-

siderable importance even apart from massage
and magnetism, and on this account it is indispensable to know the practice according to the
rules of the magnetic art, which is most simple
and can be understood by everybody.

How to practice rubbing. In magnetism there
are two kinds of rubbing, the *slow* and *rotatory.*

Slow Rubbing. Slow rubbing is practiced
gently by following, in a downward direction, the
lines of the nerves and muscles. The hand must
be flat out, the fingers separated and slightly
turned in, so that the entire hand to the tips of
the fingers drags or presses on the part you are
working. In drawing along your hand you must
agitate all the joints in exercising a series of
slight pressings, as if, from place to place, you
wanted to detach and then carry along something
adhering to the skin or subcutaneous parts. Slow
rubbing is stimulating. Practiced on the inter-
ested muscles and from the spine to the sternum,
it is very efficacious against atonic affections of
the chest, and especially against oppression es-
soufflement, and the very painful attacks of asth-
ma. Practiced on the sides of the body and on
the legs, right down to the feet, it exerts an effect
like that of the long passes.

Rotatory Rubbing. Is performed in describing concentric circles with the palm of the hand,
just stroking on the clothes the part you wish to

activate. The effect of rotatory rubbing is exciting, especially when practiced from left to right, i. e., in the direction in which the hands of a watch move.. It is practiced over all parts of the body, but preferably on the plexus and the vertebral column, for combating atony of the nervous system, on the head, liver, stomach, intestine, and the back, whenever these organs lack activity; against gout, humors, obstructions and engorgements of all kinds. The masseur always practices frictions on the naked skin, whereas the magnetizer does so over the clothes. I would observe that the rubbing which does the most good is that which is practiced gently, almost without muscular force, and only by handling and stroking.

CHAPTER VI.

BREATHING—BREATH OF LIFE—HOT INSUFFLATION—
How TO PRACTICE IT—RESTORING THE DEAD TO
LIFE—COLD INSUFFLATION—HOW PERFORMED—
ITS VALUE.

Breath is the most apparent sign of material life. After having formed man from the dust of the earth, the Creator animated it, Moses tells us, in breathing into it the *breath of life*. When the soul abandons to the earth the perishable body it has nourished, our usual expression is that we have rendered our *last breath*. It is by the breath that the Cevennes prophets communicated the prophetic inspiration to those who, up till then, had escaped the influence of that religious enthusiasm, and by which some exorcists healed the possessed.

When we breathe freely we offer all the appearance of health, while shortness of breath and difficulty in breathing offen show general weakness and almost always a want of equilibrium in the vital functions. The lungs, which are the organs of respiration, are therefore in a robust and healthy man an important source of vital energy which he can utilize for the good of his fellow man, weakened or enfeebled by sickness. The annals of history relate many cases where unexpected cures have been brought about by breathing. Arnobe tells us that, from time immemorial, there were among the Egyptians men who, by means of touching and breathing, triumphed over diseases which medicine had been unable to relieve. Mercklin tells us that a young child was brought back to life by the breath of an old woman *(Tractatus medico-physic, p. 116)*.

In the work already mentioned Peter Borel says that in his time (1628-1689) there still existed in India a sect of doctors who cured sicknesses by insufflation. The same author relates that a domestic, returning from a voyage and finding his master dead, tenderly and repeatedly embraced the inanimate body. Thinking he still discovered some signs of life, he breathed his breath with persistence into it in order to reanimate it, and at the end of some time the master returned to life. "Is it astonishing," he adds, "that the breath of man should produce such results when we read that God breathed into the body of Adam to give him life? It is a fraction of this divine breath which even today can bring back health to the sick."

Delancre, the celebrated demonomaniac, says: "There are also certain persons in Spain called *insalmadores,* who heal by the saliva and by the breath."

The action of breathing has always held a high place in therapeutics, and even today the physician employs, concurrently with repeated drawing of the tongue, insufflation from mouth to mouth against asphyxia and especially against apparent death of new-born infants. Therefore, there is in this action a considerable source of energy which may be attributed to two chief causes; 1, a mechanical cause; 2, a magnetic cause, which concur reciprocally to produce the effects observed. Magnetizers, who have always employed the action of breathing with success, give this process the name of *insufflation,* and they practice, as the case may be, *hot insufflation* and *cold insufflation.*

Hot Insufflation. This is the most powerful of all magnetic processes. From the point of view of modality its action is positive, but on account of its force, it is exciting, or at least stimulating, on all parts of the body.

How to practice hot insufflation. This insufflation is practiced in two different ways—by contact and at a distance. In the first case, the lips slightly apart, leaving the mouth half open, are placed upon the skin, or better still, upon some light piece of clothing covered with a clean towel or handkerchief; and in pressing, so that the breath does not escape, and as if it could penetrate the skin and the subcutaneous tissues, you force it energetically by a prolonged expiration. In the second case you breathe at a distance of half an inch or an inch, just as you do in winter to warm your hands. This insufflation can also be practiced with a tube, one end of which you apply to the part you wish to act upon, but better results are always obtained by the first method.

After three or four hot insufflations practiced in this way on the part of the body or diseased organ, the patient experiences an internal warmth which powerfully increases the organic activity.

We at once understand the importance of this process for cases of atony of the viscera, paralysis, humors, obstruction and stagnation. Operated on the heart, syncope ceases immediately in almost every instance. But when its action is too exciting there is danger in some cases, and for this reason it must never be employed where there are deep wounds nor against aneurism of the heart and the aorta, nor for pulmonary phthisis in the third degree of its development.

How to practice cold insufflation. This is always practiced at a distance, in blowing as if to put out a candle. Being negative, its action is the opposite to that of hot insufflation. Instead of exciting, it is calming, especially on the front of the body. Practiced on the forehead, it quickly awakens the magnetic sleeper and clears a heavy and congested head.

CHAPTER VII.

FIXITY OF GAZE — FASCINATION — THE EVIL EYE — HARSH MEASURES OF INFLUENCING OTHERS.

The eye exercises a powerful magnetic influence, and we all know that there are some persons with a slow and fascinating eye whose concentrated gaze we find it difficult to support. It is by the power of the eye that the dog arrests the partridge, and the serpent fascinates the bird and attracts it to him. With the tamer the eye constitutes the weapon which has the strongest hold on the wild animals of a menagerie. As sickness can, in a measure, be communicated by waves from one person to another, just the same as health, it has been supposed, not without reason, that the gaze of some persons produces a disagreeable effect, and the name of *evil eye* has been applied to those who exercise or are capable of exercising this power over their fellow man. Exaggerating this property of the eye considered in its worst aspect, we may easily understand that at the time sorcery flourished, there were persons who believed in the power of the *jettatores,* i. e., certain sorcerers who were supposed to throw lots by the evil action of the eye. If we admit that the eye of certain persons can influence others in an unpleasant or obnoxious way, it is clear that the kind and benevolent gaze of a sympathetic friend in robust health can have a salutary effect. The gaze *allowed to fall softly* on a patient facing you at a distance of two or three yards exercises a deep calmative effect, and may be employed with success in acute affections and also when there is enervation, irritability and excitation of the nervous system. Fixity of gaze may be used by itself, but it is generally advisable to employ it in conjunction with other modes of magnetization, i. e., with application, imposition or rubbing, and you should allow your gaze to descend gently to the parts you are operating on, so as to obtain increased results. In longitudinal and long passes your gaze must follow the movement of your hands. The gaze must fall softly on the patient or on the parts to be calmed, because if you look with a harsh gaze, indicating your determination to act energetically, instead of being calmative, the effect would be stimulating and the desired result would not be obtained. As to staring into the patient's eyes for the purpose of fascinating, it is a harsh process, the magnetiser abandons it to the hypnotiser for sending his patients to sleep.

CHAPTER VIII.

INTERMEDIATE MAGNETISM—MAGNETIZING OBJECTS— SECRET OF MAGNETISM IS VIBRATION—MAGNETIZING WATER—ITS EXTRAORDINARY EFFECT—HOW TO MAGNETIZE FLUIDS.

In all times and with nearly all peoples a preservative and curative virtue has attached to certain objects, such as phylacteries, amulets, talismans, coins, and objects blessed or consecrated, which had received an influence they were supposed to transmit to those wearing them. Philters and certain noxious objects could transmit the evil influence they had received and could carry with them the principle, the cause of sinister passions, sickness and misfortune. Making allowance for exaggeration, there is, in traditions, customs and superstitions that antiquity has handed down to us, a considerable portion of truth which official science has not recognized. In any case, it is demonstrated that, to use an expression of the old magnetizers, almost all the bodies of nature are charged, saturated more or less, with the magnetic agent, that they retain this saturation for a certain period, and that, while it lasts, an action of some kind may be observed. This property of the magnetic force of settling in various bodies has been made use of for *indirect* or *intermediate magnetization,* i. e., practiced by the aid of certain bodies magnetized beforehand. With the wave theory, it would be more rational to say that the vibratory movement of the atoms of the magnetizing body is transmitted to the atoms of the body magnetized; that a certain equilibrium tends to set in, and that the two bodies try to vibrate in unison. It is then that the magnetic property of the one is communicated to the other. As words do not alter things, I will continue to use the expressions formerly employed, because they explain in a better manner the results obtained.

All bodies are not charged with magnetism to the same extent; we might say that all have not the same magnetic capacity. Liquids are, of all bodies, those which absorb it in the greatest degree and retain it the longest. Cotton and woolen stuffs, glass and metals also possess great magnetic capacity. Metals, which have their own polarity, are even valuable auxiliaries, for some become saturated with only positive fluid, while others only take negative fluids. Thus with them we can bring to bear on a determined point of the surface of the body an exclusively calming or exciting action. Silk can only be charged with much difficulty, and may therefore be considered as an insulator. It can be used to advantage for covering magnetized objects to preserve them against contact with the air, which gradually discharges them. Magnetizers attach great importance to magnetized water for patients to drink, either pure or mixed with wine, at meals. It is also advantageously employed for injections, irrigation of the stomach, for lotions and compresses. We can, nay, we should, in the course of a treatment, magnetize most of the food. Terrestrial magnetism, light, heat, chemical action, sound, and movement may be employed in magnetizing the various substances and divers objects which serve as intermediaries between the magnetizer and the patient, but the most powerful and practical mediums are, first, human magnetism, and then the magnet.

Human Magnetism. In order to magnetize a piece of stuff, a sheet of glass or metal or any object, it is held in one or other of the hands according as you wish to magnetize positively or negatively, or else alternately in both hands, if mixed magnetism is desired. Then you execute passes or digital imposition, and after that, insufflation. At the end of five or six minutes the saturation is complete; the object is magnetized. To magnetize liquids you place them in a vase, basin, cup or glass, and execute passes and digital imposition with either or both hands. If the liquid is destined for external use, you can put your hands in it and practice hot insufflation on it. According to the quantity of liquid to be magnetized, complete saturation requires from four to ten minutes.

Magnetism of the Magnet. A horseshoe, or any other magnet, can be employed, but the magnetic bar I use is preferable on account of its accessories, as shown in the adjoining figure. To magnetize a piece of cloth, a sheet of glass or metal or any object, you place it in contact with one of the poles of the magnet, or with both successively. You can dispense with placing the object to be magnetized in direct contact; all that is necessary is to place it in the field of its action.

To magnetize a liquid you can likewise place the vase containing it in the field of action of the magnet, but it is preferable to plunge into the liquid the silver needles at the end of the conducting wires of the bar. Saturation is completed in from ten to twenty minutes, according to the quantity of liquid to be magnetized. I would here state to users of this bar that in order to obtain from it the maximum of magnetic action, it is necessary to use it horizontally in the direction from east to west, the X pole towards the first, the — pole towards the second, and that when not in use it should, if it is to retain its force, be suspended horizontally, or placed on a bureau or tall piece of furniture in the direction of the meridian, the X pole toward the north. An im-

portant remark may be made here. A liquid or any object charged with human magnetism retains its property for a long time, but charged with the magnet or any other mode of magnetism it loses very rapidly, so that after eight or ten days there remains no perceptible effect. The action of fire scarcely weakens human magnetism, but it destroys almost entirely that of the magnet and the other bodies or forces of nature. Consequently you must not heat to the boiling point any water but that magnetized by human magnetism. To give an idea of the therapeutic value of magnetized water, even by the aid of a magnet, I think it instructive to reproduce here a personal observation. A few years ago, at the clinic of the *Ecole pratique de Magnetisme et de Massage,* attended Thursdays and Sundays by twenty to thirty-five patients each seance, I proposed to them to give them water magnetized by the action of the magnet, so as to hasten their cure. .I did not praise the properties of this water, remaining satisfied with saying that I had often observed its good effects on patients. They almost all accepted my generous offer, and in exchange for their promise to render me an account of the effects they might observe, I handed a bottle of it to each one. The water, placed in a great tub in my laboratory, was subjected for a whole night to the action of a horseshoe magnet set at 240 pounds. I had the patients' bottles filled during the seance, and then returned to them, so that they could employ the contents at home. Those affected with sores, weak eyes, or skin diseases used it in lotions and compresses ; those suffering from organic complaints took it internally, pure or mixed with table wine, while others utilized it for gargling, injections, etc.

Right from the start the most salutory effects were noticed by nearly all the patients. In internal complaints digestion was better, appetites more regular, discomfort ceased, pains diminished; and in those suffering from constipation, laxative effects were observed without any apparent exterior cause. In internal maladies the sores healed better, the weak eyes were sensibly stronger, and all the patients claimed to have in the water one of the most valuable remedies they had ever used; so that, at each sitting, not one missed bringing his bottle, some even coming for a supply between the seances. A good·many were so satisfied with the water that they sent for it and discontinued coming to the clinic to be magnetized.

This first part of the experiment lasted two months. I listened attentively to the observations of each one without sharing their enthusiasm, because I thought their imagination played, if not the principal part, at least considerably helped the real effects naturally resulting from the action of the magnetized liquid. But I had no difficulty in deciding between imagination and genuine effect, and the following account of what I did will form the second part of the experiment. One fine morning, without saying anything, I handed the same water to each patient, but without its having been magnetized. If im-

agination played any part in the production of
the phenomena observed these should have continued to occur almost in the same way because,
not knowing that I was experimenting, their
confidence in me was the same. But it was not
so. At the following seance, and without my
asking them anything to avoid any suspicion, at
least two-thirds of the patients told me they had
not found in the water that particular flavor it usually had, and that its effect had been nil or in-
significant. In a few, whose imagination might
have helped the effect of the remedy, say in a
fourth of the patients, there were some good results; but all were quite sure that if the water
of the last seance was magnetized, it was less
so than that of previous seances. I told them it
ought to be to the same extent, and that if the
effects appeared less considerable, it could only
be owing to some fault of their own when using
it. Admitting this reason, they again willingly
took away another bottle (which was no more
magnetized than the one before). Whatever
remained of imagination disappeared completely,
for all the patients were absolutely unanimous
in saying the water had produced no effect at all.
I advised them to continue with it, in giving the
most suggestive arguments, but only a few con-
sented to keep on with the trial, which, it must
not be forgotten, had been producing excellent

results for two months. At the fifth sitting, being satisfied with the result, I intended to continue the experiment, giving the patients fresh
arguments to try to get them to take some water which, this time, was more magnetized than
ever, for I had left it under the action of the
magnet for twenty-four hours. All my arguments were in vain; not one of them would take
it; they all told me it had *no longer any effect
on them*.

I was disappointed, for I was very desirous of
continuing the experiment so well begun, but although fairly conclusive, it remained unfinished.

It is necessary to note here that (without its
chemical condition being modified) most patients
find a particular flavor in magnetized water, enabling them to distinguish it from the same water not magnetized. Magnetized with the right
hand or with the positive pole (X) of the magnet, it takes an acidulated taste which renders it
cool and pleasant; while magnetized with the
left hand or with the negative (—) pole of the
magnet, it has an alkaline flavor, rendering it
tasteless and unpleasant. The first excites the
functions of the stomach; the second diminishes
them. Magnetized with both hands, or with
both poles of the magnet, it possessed mixed properties which suit most palates.

CHAPTER IX.

THE PURPOSE OF MAGNETISM — TO CALM AND TO STIMULATE—IMPORTANCE OF KNOWING THE HOW AND THE WHY—DIRECTIONS FOR USE.

We know experimentally that the human body is polarized like a magnet, and that the action of one on the other of their opposite poles diminishes organic activity, that is, *calms,* whereas that of their same poles augments this activity, that is, *excites.* But as the action of all the methods I have just indicated is not entirely explained by polarity, it is advisable to give here a few instructions as to the manner of employing them, classing them according to their energy.

To calm. In a severe disease, with the patient agitated, delirious, in intense fever, or suffering considerably, you must calm as much as possible. In order to do so, place yourself, at first, at the foot of the bed; let your gaze fall gently on the chest or on the region of the stomach, and, if possible, apply your hands to his feet or on the lower part of the legs. This is the most calmative method the magnetizer can use. At the end of ten or thirty minutes, as the case may be, the fever and the heat of the body sensibly diminish, agitation ceases, the delirium disappears, the pain is lessened and the patient enjoys a rest he may not have felt for a long time. This first result obtained, you may wait awhile, or continue the action in using methods calmative in a lesser degree. In the latter case, standing at the patient's side, you make heteronomous applications on the various parts of the body, and especially on the seat of the disease; then you terminate the seance with longitudinal passes practiced very slowly from the head to the epigastrium, and then from the chest to the extremities.

If you have to deal with one of those numerous cases characterised by an augmentation of the organic activity, by pain, fever or any excitation in a patient who is not in bed, you must calm, but in a lesser degree than in the preceding case. In order to do so, and either standing or sitting in front of your patient, you begin by making applications on the hands, on the thighs, then on the different parts of the body, and especially on the seat of the pain. You then follow with longitudinal passes practiced very slowly at first, from the head to the epigastrium, then from the chest as far as the extremities; after that, longitudinal passes practiced faster, from the head to the extremities. You terminate the seance with long passes from head to foot, so as to regularize the action. Neuralgic pains are calmed particularly by application of the hands, to the exclusion of all other methods.

A hot, heavy and congested head is soon cleared

under the action of cold insufflation on the forehead, by transversal passes practiced on the head and all around the upper part of the body, by the application of the hands on the knees and on the thighs, as far as the extremities, by long passes; and especially, standing at your patient's left, by the application of your left hand to his forehead, the fingers extended, while your right hand executes slow rubbing on the vertebral column, from the base of the neck to the lower part of the back.

To excite. It is a good plan always to begin your action without any roughness. Being seated in front of your patient, you first apply your hands on his in a heteronomous position, your knees against his knees and your feet against his feet, in order to establish what former magnetizers used to call *the rapport;* then with your hands you make isonomous applications on the various parts of the body, and more especially on the seat of the pain. Then longitudinal passes practiced in front of the patient, as if to calm, followed by palmar imposition, digital imposition, and if you need considerable excitation, rotary, or even perforating, imposition. You finish up with slow and rotatory rubbings, and, if necessary, hot insufflation.

In a great number of cases where it is necessary to stimulate one or all of the functions, it is advisable to excite at first, so as to calm afterward. I need not enter into fuller details on this subject, for with a little common sense the reader will sufficiently understand which are the methods he can best combine in order to obtain the greatest amount of beneficial action he can hope for.

www.ingramcontent.com/pod-product-compliance
Lightning Source LLC
Chambersburg PA
CBHW070200290526
45789CB00002B/850